C000184158

Provincetown
SINCE WORLD WAR II
Carnival at Land's End

DEBRA LAWLESS

Charleston London

THE
History
PRESS

Published by The History Press
Charleston, SC 29403
www.historypress.net

Copyright © 2014 by Debra Lawless
All rights reserved

Front cover, top: Detail of a painting by Deane Folsom II.
Back cover, bottom: Painting by Deane Folsom Sr.

First published 2014

Manufactured in the United States

ISBN 978.1.60949.476.6

Library of Congress CIP data applied for.

Notice: The information in this book is true and complete to the best of our knowledge. It is offered without guarantee on the part of the author or The History Press. The author and The History Press disclaim all liability in connection with the use of this book.

All rights reserved. No part of this book may be reproduced or transmitted in any form whatsoever without prior written permission from the publisher except in the case of brief quotations embodied in critical articles and reviews.

To the memories of my mother, Barbara Aaronson, and my friend Stuart Stearns once again.

Contents

Acknowledgements

Many generous people helped me with this project. I thank Katherine Baltivik, Jeannette de Beauvoir, Alice Brock, Robert Harrison and Andrea Sawyer for graciously talking to me about their lives in Provincetown. The paintings and photographs contributed by the talented Folsom family—Deane Sr., Oris and Deane II—are invaluable gifts to this book. Deane Sr. studied under Philip Malicoat, who was himself a student of Charles Webster Hawthorne. Deane Sr. is known for his nostalgic train paintings and has been represented by several Provincetown galleries. Oris studied under Malicoat and also under Henry Hensche, Hawthorne's assistant, who continued teaching in Provincetown after Hawthorne's death. Deane II is both a photographer and an artist, and I thank him, too, for helping select his parents' work.

I also thank Carolyn Brault Seefer for her wonderful photographs of "Bear Week." I thank the staffs of the Brewster Ladies Library in Brewster and the Eldredge Public Library in Chatham and my kind friends in the Nickerson Family Association, especially Ben, Brian, Edmond, Gail, Ron and Karen, Scott and Anne Nickerson; Jinny Devine; and Ken and Judy Needham. I thank my colleagues at the *Cape Cod Chronicle*, the Cape Cod Writers Center and on the editorial board of the *Journal of the Cape Cod Genealogical Society*.

Writing a book for several months in "solitary confinement" is not easy! I am blessed with a wonderful circle of lovely friends and cousins whom I treasure for provocative discussions and much encouragement:

ACKNOWLEDGEMENTS

Patti Aaronson and Diane Iniguez, William Beinecke, Jan Bilhuber, Laurie Blanchard, Ellen Borden, John Bullock, Ellen C. Collins, Cecilia Deane, Roger and Adrienne Denk, Caitlin and Joanne Doggart, Betsy Freedman Doherty, Eric Dorsey, Karl and Brenda Dunakin, Elizabeth Berrigan Dunlop, Christina and Julia Evola, Gloria Freeman, Leah Goat, Mary Ann Gray, Andy Miller Hill, Fred Howard, Paul and Susan Huling, Marilyn Hunter, Doug and Heather Karn, Robin Kew, Elizabeth Laufer, George Lawless III, Babs Lidbeck, Eric Linder, Judy Llewellyn, Kathrine Lovell, David Olsen, Ursula Panzarella, Barbara Pierce, Catherine Saar, Mary Siqueiros, Jo-Anne Sliva, Sarah Soule, Mike Watkiss and Jan and Ted Whittaker. Each one of you contributed to this book in some way. My dear friend Stuart Stearns died as I was writing this book; it was a privilege to spend ten years in his exuberant company, and I will miss him at book events.

I thank the very capable staff of The History Press and, in particular, my editor, Katie Orlando, for her guidance on this project.

I also thank my husband, John, for his unwavering love—not to mention proofreading—through four books.

Finally, I nod to my Boston University City Room professor Jon Klarfeld, who taught me long ago to be skeptical with the words "interesting, if true."

1
The War Years and After, 1939-1949

The town withdrew into itself, and the cold, which was nothing remarkable when measured with a thermometer…was nonetheless a cold sea air filled with the bottomless chill that lies at the cloistered heart of ghost stories.
—Norman Mailer on Provincetown in the autumn

The Black Flash

Some said he was searching for his ship lost off Race Point.

Others said he had a date with the devil at Peaked Hill.

While few had actually seen him, everyone knew someone who knew someone who had seen him lurking in these narrow streets of Provincetown at the very tip of Cape Cod.

They called him the Black Flash. He materialized out of the dark and jumped over ten-foot hedges with no trouble at all, as though he had "chair springs on his feet."

He stood seven feet tall, clad in a black hood and a long black cape. His speech was "guttural."

When he perched on a windowsill on Bangs Street, the elderly woman on the other side of the window drove him away with her screams.

He chased two youths thirteen blocks in the dark. And Captain Phineus Blackstrap claimed he had never seen him "without he's gnawing away at

The Black Flash chased his victims through the narrow, deserted streets in the weeks before Halloween 1939. *Painting by Oris Folsom.*

a skully-jo," that peculiar Provincetown delicacy made of dried, hardened cod in stick form.

By October 1939, the artists, tourists and summer folk had all gone home, leaving the four thousand or so Portuguese and Yankee residents to be most purely themselves in their town here at land's end. Seasonal businesses closed, and the streets were largely deserted after hours as the wind off the harbor whipped past the houses grown unkempt since the Great Depression. Artist Robert Motherwell, who came to town a couple of years later, remembered a poor town with "peeling paint, askew shutters, holes in roofs, primitive stoves and occasional kerosene lamps."[1] Whoever, or whatever, the Black Flash was, it was true that Provincetown's children had trouble sleeping in their own beds with a bogeyman loose. They had so much trouble, in fact, that police chief Anthony P. Tarvers, who said the Black Flash was nothing but a lot of hooey, begged to be left alone long enough to get some sleep himself.

Halloween, the night before All Saints' Day, is a magical night. Some would say it's black magic that's afoot. On this night, the veil between the worlds of the living and the dead is supposed to be at its thinnest. In

Provincetown, some rascals usually stole the town crier's bell. And it was during these days before Halloween that the Black Flash menaced the town. Halloween that year was celebrated at a party thrown in Provincetown Town Hall by the police department. The one-dollar prize for best costume went to three-year-old Manuel Jason Jr.—he dressed as the Black Flash.

Just one year after Orson Wells, with his radio broadcast of *The War of the Worlds*, terrified the nation into believing aliens had landed in a New Jersey field, news of Provincetown's Black Flash was broadcast on radios nationwide. Whatever was real and whatever was fancy, it was true that darkness fell a little earlier every day and that in this small town, "in too little space, with just the same faces to look at every morning, afternoon, and evening," it was easy to let one's imagination run wild when a gust of salty wind crackled dried leaves in the dark.

Weird stories take on lives of their own in Provincetown. In 1886, town crier George Washington Ready said he saw a six-eyed sea serpent reeking of sulfur near Herring Pond. Just a few months before the Black Flash arrived, in January 1939, an eighteen-foot skeleton with seventy-one vertebrae washed ashore. Crowds gathered at the Coast Guard station to gasp over it. While many believed it was the skeleton of Ready's sea serpent, a Harvard scientist declared it a "basking shark."

In 1939, the skeleton of what was believed to be a sea monster was displayed here at the U.S. Coast Guard Station at Race Point for all to admire and photograph. *Collection of the author.*

The word "weird" cropped up frequently. The dunes, often compared with those of the Sahara Desert, were said to be "weirdly beautiful." The famous marine artist Frederick Waugh, toiling away with his brushes in his West End studio on Commercial Street, was said to devote "considerable time to spinning weird and unusual tales" for children. His nickname was "Wizard."

Like a good fish story, the tale of the Black Flash got bigger with every telling. As the *Advocate* remarked later about loose talk during wartime in Provincetown, "We conjure up weird ideas about what we figure is going to happen, then think about it a bit—not over much—and the next thing we know the ideas have become facts. Away goes the story with every relayer adding a bit."[2]

It was true, too, that in this town where the houses were built close together on famously narrow streets, an arsonist had been hard at work during one of the town's lowest periods, the Great Depression. And the mysterious fires had started up again during that fall of the Black Flash, with mattresses used as kindling and women such as Georgiana Webster, widow of the painting instructor E. Ambrose Webster, targeted in their grief.

It was also true that most everyone was tense that fall of 1939, as the world watched the Germans bomb and burn their way through Poland and no one knew if America would be tugged into another war.

Whatever the Black Flash was—a gremlin or a quartet of mischievous boys, as the police believed—it disappeared as quickly as it came. Yet it left a pocket of fear in people's hearts.

The Beginning of the Art Colony

Let's get it straight from the outset: The Pilgrims landed first in Provincetown. They stayed for thirty-four days before sailing off to Plymouth. Although Plymouth, in the nearly three intervening centuries, had done much to steal Provincetown's glory, the Pilgrim Monument, dedicated in 1910, was designed to settle the matter.

Some say it was the summer of 1899, when artist Charles Webster Hawthorne arrived, that changed the course of Provincetown, a fishing village turned to the sea rather than to the rest of Cape Cod. The vicious storm known as the Portland Gale, two days after Thanksgiving 1898, had destroyed much of the town's infrastructure of wharves. When Hawthorne looked around Provincetown and noticed its light—"a jumble of color in the intense sunlight, accentuated by the brilliant blue of the harbor"—he would be only one of the

Artists were drawn to this fishing village due to the abundance of affordable housing. Here is an early view of the East End of Commercial Street. *Collection of the author.*

first in a century of painters, sculptors, photographers and poets who would come to Provincetown, at land's end, to work in that special light.

Within a couple of years, Hawthorne's school, based in a big barn on Miller Hill Road, was well established and attracting art students who roomed in the town's houses and lived on the cheap on fish. While the town remained, at heart, a fishing village with a Portuguese flavor, the *Mayflower* crowd; the vast numbers of serious painters, writers and intellectuals; and the burgeoning gay population made it into a miniature melting pot. Tourism boomed during the summers of the '10s, '20s and '30s with multitudes disembarking every day from the Boston day boat. By the eve of World War II, Provincetown was a famous tourist destination.

"Peace for Our Time"

It was a tense year, 1939.

Perhaps the best portrait we have of Provincetown during the four first decades of the twentieth century is provided by journalist Mary Heaton

Vorse in her charming book *Time and the Town*, published in 1941. Vorse bought her house at 466 Commercial Street overlooking the harbor in 1908 and, working as a journalist traveling the world, used the house as her base. Now sixty-four and a grandmother, she spent the winter of 1939 quietly at home, perhaps putting the finishing touches on *Time and the Town* and visiting with her daughter Mary Ellen and her grandchild, who popped in and out of the house. "That winter I was especially conscious of the town and how long I had been here. Boys who had played in the yard as babies were now coming to dinner with their wives," Vorse wrote in *Time and the Town*.[3] She also took in a refugee who was writing a book on Leonardo da Vinci.

Just the previous September, British prime minister Neville Chamberlain had traveled to Germany to meet with Chancellor Adolf Hitler and came back speaking of "peace for our time." This was an era when it seemed that the world could tilt toward either war or peace. After the Germans annexed the Sudetenland in October 1938, everyone waited through a tense period like a lull before a storm. "People turned their radios to news more than ever," Vorse observed.

In March 1939, Henry C. Hampe, a German native, addressed an audience of nearly forty at the Anchor and Ark Club about his recent travels through the "new Germany." During his five weeks there, he "saw nothing to bear out stories of persecution of Jews by the Nazis." A roast lamb supper was then served to club members. The following month, the arctic explorer Donald Baxter MacMillan, sixty-four, who lived on the water side of Commercial Street a few doors down from Vorse, planned to embark on his eighteenth voyage aboard the schooner *Bowdoin* and hoped "that war clouds will pass," the *Advocate* reported on April 13, 1939. MacMillan and his young wife, Miriam, thirty-three, had recently celebrated their fourth wedding anniversary. In the years to come, MacMillan would be increasingly celebrated as the final survivor of Admiral Robert E. Peary's 1909 expedition to the North Pole.

As the winter drew to a close, Vorse was eager to journey to Europe to view firsthand what was happening. Between April and September 1939, Vorse traveled through France, Germany and Switzerland and on to Belgrade and Budapest, reporting events in Europe for the *New Republic*, *New York Times* and other publications.[4]

Finally, on September 1, when Germany invaded Poland, this strange time of waiting for war, this sham "peace for our time," ended. A week later, Vorse sailed home. France fell in the spring of 1940. And although the war was still "over there," paranoia nevertheless gripped Provincetown. Under the *Advocate*'s November 29 headline, "Hitler Is Trying to Sway Cape-Tip," there followed a story about the sinister propaganda letter that Anthony C. Tarvers of Commercial Street had received, "written by an unmistakable Teutonic hand." Others received printed literature designed to turn them toward the Fuehrer. Just as it had been in the previous war, a devious kind of terror machine was at play.

A Bitter Winter

In January 1940, the navy tugboat *Navajo* arrived in Provincetown Harbor for trials. Later, the tugs *Cherokee* and *Seminole* would arrive, the *Advocate* reported on January 4, 1940. The winter began so frigid that for the first time in four years, men cut ice at Crawley's Pond to supply the town's freezers. "It is expected that 70 or more men will be employed with the harvesting of the ice which is between seven and eight inches thick with no break in the cold yet in sight."[5] Skating, too, was marvelous.

On Valentine's Day came a fierce blizzard. The storm began with "an angry, darkening sky that shone dull green" in the surf, the *Advocate* reported. Winds from the northeast drove sand, sleet and snow. In fact, the fierce wind ripped shingles from the roof of town hall with such force that one of them cut through a parked car. At least twenty-five men and women slept in chairs in town hall overnight, unable to brave the storm. Along Beach Point, winds up to eighty miles an hour were recorded. Tumbling telephone poles were held up by guy wires.

When dawn broke the following morning, it was clear that the "famous old Wharf Theatre" at 83 Commercial Street was a "twisted and torn jumble, pulled this way and that by the force of the wind." For the last few summers, the theater had been operated by Neil McFee Skinner and his wife, Edith. Snow everywhere was piled up to six feet and deeper, with snowbound cars scattered everywhere, making the streets impassable. Rail service was down. During the week that followed, strong winds and heavy seas battered the theater.

Theater in Provincetown had a distinguished pedigree. The reclusive and as-yet-unknown playwright Eugene O'Neill arrived in Provincetown in 1916 and lived there off and on during World War I. In July 1916, O'Neill's *Bound East for Cardiff* premiered in Mary Heaton Vorse's fish shed on Lewis Wharf. Theater had come to Provincetown the previous year, when Vorse; Susan Glaspell, who would win a Pulitzer Prize in 1931; Susan's husband, George

During the fierce Valentine's Day blizzard of 1940, many were forced to seek overnight shelter in Provincetown Town Hall. *Photo by the author.*

Cram Cook; Neith Boyce; Hutchins Hapgood; John Reed; Louise Bryant and others began reading plays in a Commercial Street living room.

In 1916, the Provincetown Players moved into Vorse's fish house, which seated ninety. Yet after only two seasons, the Provincetown Players moved to Greenwich Village, in New York, where the group performed until 1929.

In 1923, Mary Bicknell organized the Wharf Players, with Frank Shay as director. (Shay later broke away and organized his own group, the Barnstormers, which staged plays in an old barn on Bradford Street.) In 1925, the Wharf Players completed construction of the Wharf Theatre, which was now gone.[6]

The *Advocate* spoke out, a few days after the Wharf Theatre was destroyed, on the need to restore the luster of summer theater in Provincetown. As a whole, the influence of Provincetown's theater "on plays, theatre and on the interest of theatre-goers throughout the nation has been tremendous," the paper crowed, adding that a strong summer theater would increase the town's summer revenues.

"Oh, It Was a Golden Time, That Summer..."

Just before the Fourth of July 1940, the town jail was condemned. "What no lace curtains! No running water! No bellhop service! No radio in every cell!" a columnist for the *Advocate* sniped on July 3. "Maybe the town fathers should make a deal to house the drunks in some hotel." Not that Provincetown was in the midst of a crime wave. In the entire year of 1940, there were 118 arrests, with most crimes having something to do with drunkenness. The town also had one arson, one statutory rape, one vagrant and, interestingly, ten "insane persons" who were committed to one of four state hospitals.

Perhaps a greater threat came from measles. The measles epidemic was waning early in the summer of 1940, when Tennessee Williams boarded a train in New York on the first leg of his journey to Provincetown, "a place I'd barely heard of," he recalled in his 1975 *Memoirs*. This was to be the first of the four summers—1940, 1941, 1944 and 1947—in which he would set foot in Provincetown.

Williams was twenty-nine years old; in four years, he would be acclaimed for *The Glass Menagerie*, but as yet, he was an unknown playwright. In Boston, he caught the daily ferry to Provincetown and, once in town, checked into a rooming house full of young people. That first evening, he managed to

Captain Jack's wharf today. When Tennessee Williams stayed here in the 1940s, the rickety wharf was home to several inexpensive, shanty-type summer rentals. *Photo by the author.*

seduce a "blond youth" as the two of them shared a swing hanging on the front porch. Soon, he had settled right in and was calling Provincetown the "frolicsome tip of the Cape."

By July, Williams had moved to a "little two-story shack" on Captain Jack's Wharf at 73 Commercial Street. Williams's housemates were Joseph Hazan, who had come to Provincetown to pose for the famous art teacher Hans Hofmann, and Kip Kiernan, a Canadian dancer with whom Williams began a love affair.

An essential key to Provincetown's ability to attract artists, writers and playwrights in their salad days lay in its abundant cheap housing. That year, the Board of Health inspected 357 rooming houses.[7] A September 3, 1937 block ad for Captain Jack's Wharf in the *Advocate* showed a sketch of the rickety wharf and its buildings and advertised, "Studios on the Sea Where Well Known People Meet and Mingle on the Gay and Happy Boardwalk." The ad went on, "Drop in before you leave and inspect the delightfully appointed studio apartments to be found there." No matter how "delightfully appointed" the apartments might have been, they had primitive waste arrangements. Until June 1942, toilets emptied through open wooden drains that poured into the West End shore. At the start of that first wartime summer of 1942, the town's well-known physician, Daniel H. Hiebert, installed two modern cement septic containers at Captain Jack's Wharf at a cost of about $500.[8]

Still, if you appreciated a room with a view—the wharf stuck out into the harbor—and you wanted to find someplace to live on the cheap, Captain Jack's Wharf could not be beat. A 1940 photograph shows people seated in Adirondack chairs, reading and chatting on the deck that ran along the individual apartments.

"Oh, it was a golden time, that summer, everyone seemed lighthearted despite the war being on!" Williams recalled in *Memoirs*. It is interesting that Williams brings the war into this quote, as it was as yet overseas and Americans were not yet playing a great role.

By mid-July, Williams's affair with Kiernan was in full throttle. Yet his carefree days with Kiernan lasted only until sometime in August, when Kiernan broke Williams's heart by telling him that a girl had warned him Williams was "turning him homosexual." Also in August, Williams met the as-yet unknown painter Jackson Pollock. "I remember him for his boisterous, just slightly drunk behavior," Williams recalled in *Memoirs*. Pollock would put Williams on his shoulders and carry him out into the water "to sport about innocently." Finally, still reeling from the shock of losing Kiernan, Williams left Provincetown for Mexico.

As he departed, Williams stood at the rail of the ferry and saw "P-town dwindling sort of dream-like behind me." Captain Jack's was "very tiny, like a pile of little sticks…My throat got awfully tight for a moment."[9]

"Darling Men," the Flagship and a Famous Visitor

After the summer season wound down, the board of trade, the precursor to the Provincetown Chamber of Commerce, met to hash over the past season's need for more parking spaces and anchorage facilities—and its "darling men." (The *Advocate* printed "darling men" in scare quotes.)[10] "They must have had a convention here this year," said one board of trade member, "and certainly more and more of them are coming here every year." Board of trade president William W. Taylor grumbled that Provincetown was getting a name as "a rendezvous for fairies."

On September 10, 1940, Frederick Waugh died, just three days short of his seventy-ninth birthday. Waugh was noted not only for his seascapes but

Everyone, including first ladies, artists and sailors, mingled in the atmospheric dory bar at the Flagship Bar & Grill, 463 Commercial Street. *Collection of the author.*

also for his mural of the Madonna and Child in the Church of Saint Mary of the Harbor, which was established in 1919 at 517 Commercial Street. Waugh was seen only infrequently around town and spent most of his time working in his West End studio. "Built of the great timbers brought in from ships wrecked on the Back Shore, supported by the 'knees' of these same ships and hung with their blocks and tackle, with great chains and other fittings, the studio is a famous spot on Cape Cod," the *Advocate* noted. Under its next owner, Hans Hofmann, the studio became even more famous.

On October 3, First Lady Eleanor Roosevelt made an unannounced visit, arriving at the wheel of her own car and accompanied by only her secretary, Malvina Thompson. The pair arrived about 5:00 p.m. and checked into the Colonial Inn. A bit later, they went to dinner at the Flagship, where the first lady was reported to eat a "Cape Cod meal" of clam chowder and fried scallops as driftwood blazed in the fireplace.

The Flagship was opened in the late 1930s by Manuel Francis "Pat" Patrick in a part of E. Ambrose Webster's former studio. (The Beachcombers' "Hulk" was attached to its back.) "Skipper Pat," as he was known, spent his spare time driving a buggy with balloon tires through Provincetown's dunes looking for flotsam and jetsam from wrecks. He decorated the restaurant with buoys and old beams from ships. When the place opened in May 1938, half the names in town showed up.[11] In May 1940, the Skipper added the famous dory bar.

For many years, it seemed that anyone who spent even a night in Provincetown traipsed through the Flagship. (First Lady Jacqueline Kennedy ate there in August 1961 accompanied by writer Gore Vidal.) "The accumulation of candle drippings in the bottles on each table has reached fantastic height and design through the years, rivaling those in the Lapin Agile," the decorator Peter Hunt noted in his cookbook. "Everybody comes here for a lobster or a steak broiled over charcoal, or for Pat's famous ham steak broiled with sliced pineapple—everybody is happy here."

When Roosevelt left the next day, she declared the town "restful and delightful."

Edmund Wilson Moves to Quiet Wellfleet

In March 1941, the critic Edmund Wilson, who had lived periodically in Provincetown in rented houses since 1920, when he visited Edna St. Vincent

In 1941, after renting houses in Provincetown for many years, literary critic Edmund Wilson bought a house down the road fourteen miles, in Wellfleet. *Photo by the author.*

Millay in her family's home in Truro, finally bought his own house. The house was on Money Hill in Wellfleet and set just a few yards back from Route 6. In buying a house in Wellfleet, Wilson followed the lead of many of his friends who sought a quieter environment than Provincetown now offered. The house he chose was a "rambling, green-shuttered, white clapboard farmhouse" built in the 1820s. Wilson bought the house from a sister-in-law of Admiral Chester Nimitz.[12]

Wilson was at this time married to his third wife, Mary McCarthy. In the summer of 1930, Wilson and his second wife, Margaret Canby, had rented the old lifesaving station at Peaked Hill Bars. While Wilson had spent a glorious summer there, the building slid into the sea several months later, on New Year's Day. The purchase of the substantial house at Money Hill represented a new stage in domesticity for Wilson.

Tennessee Williams Returns to the "Mad-House"

Tennessee Williams still loved the carnival atmosphere of Provincetown and returned in the summer of 1941, a few days before the Fourth of July. He checked into a house rented from Edith Ives Cogan at 534 Commercial Street. From the moment he arrived, it was raining, and he was unable to go swimming. He claimed that his friend Joe Hazan was playing "primitive jungle music" nonstop and that the place was a "mad-house" with a "Russian Jewess with huge buttocks and a bleeding soul, a boy recently and prematurely discharged from a mental institution," a "blond youth" and two "vaguely literary and hideous young men from the Village." So he wrote in a July 12, 1941 letter to his friend Paul Bigelow.[13] Later in the month, he told Bigelow that he would leave Provincetown were it not for his lack of funds. And just as had been true for poor artists visiting Provincetown a generation before, "we eat fish at every meal because we get it for nothing."

By the end of the month, Williams was working on "a pretty good idea for a long play based on a famous refugee artist who has established a school here." He was referring, of course, to Hans Hofmann but apparently did not complete the play.[14] A few days later, Williams left Provincetown and returned to New York.

The Summer Romance of Anais Nin

Enter Anais Nin, another European refugee, now living in New York City.

While Nin and her husband, Hugh Parker Guiler, a banker, had lived mainly in Paris for fifteen years, the pair fled to New York in the late summer of 1939. In August 1941, Nin vacationed in Provincetown, according to *Mirages: The Unexpurgated Diary of Anais Nin, 1939–1947*.[15] Nin, thirty-eight that summer, was dancing to a complicated love life. Married to Guiler, she had been having a long-term affair with Henry Miller, author of *Tropic of Capricorn*. Yet she was in love with the Marxist Gonzalo Moré, who soon followed her from Europe.

She traveled with Guiler to Provincetown and there established herself in one of the many guesthouses. (Just down the road in Wellfleet was her former lover Edmund Wilson.) Nin and Guiler cycled to the beach, where they picnicked, swam and lay in the sun. On August 8, Guiler left, and Nin wrote, "I dressed myself in my most becoming costume…and walked down the street to see how many men would turn their heads, and all of them did."

Despite the many lovers in her life, Nin was on the prowl, and she noted, "Provincetown—this is no place in which to find new passion!" A night owl, Nin added that by 11:00 p.m. the town is "quite dead." She and Moré, who was staying in separate lodgings, went to the Flagship Bar and drank three whiskeys each.

Later, Nin broke a dinner date with Virginia Holton Admiral, a poet and painter, and Robert De Niro Sr., an abstract expressionist painter. The couple, who had met in Hans Hofmann's class, was married that December and became the parents of actor Robert De Niro in 1943. That evening, Nin was hunting for a man she had spotted at the bar of the Flagship, "a blond Nordic Viking." He was a Viennese opera singer, Edward Graeffe, who had come to America to debut as Siegfried at the Metropolitan.

Nin informs us that "the homosexuals have all tried to interest him," yet she was the one to win him. It is "so marvelous to reach for your dream when you are outside of the nightclub and you hear the music and you are locked out, not dancing, you are alone in a room watching the candlelight of the Flagship, but knowing tomorrow you will be inside, dancing, with a new lover."

Nin soon entered into a sexual relationship with Graeffe. Following a long tradition of trysts in the dunes, Nin and Graeffe made love "behind the

Provincetown's dunes have long been a trysting spot, as Anais Nin discovered. *Painting by Deane Folsom Sr.*

beach, hidden by the grasses." They were apparently unafraid of tick bites and sunburn.

Guiler returned for Labor Day weekend, and he and Nin went back to New York after a final dinner at the Flagship.

While Nin might have been treated regally in Provincetown, at least one sailor off one of the many ships in the harbor complained that although townsfolk were willing to take the sailors' money, they also treated them "like dirt."

The sailors went into one of the "joints," only to be steered "into a hole by ourselves. We are not good enough to sit in the main room. All we are good for is to defend these dumps if an enemy comes," the sailor complained in an anonymous letter to the *Advocate* on August 21, 1941. "And while we're not good enough some fairy at the piano sings songs only for a sporting house." The *Advocate*, almost always a civic booster, defended Provincetown's restaurants and bars, saying that in most, "sailors are not only welcome but highly respected as well."

As it turned out, the summer of 1941 was to be Provincetown's final busy summer for several years.

"Festering Piles of Putrefaction"

Perhaps because she was so self-absorbed, Nin did not mention anything in her diary about garbage strewn on the beach, about loathsome odors, about witnessing "some large bone being worried by dogs, while a bit of offal and fat flip-flopped with the tide," as Mary Heaton Vorse so memorably worded it. In Nin's Provincetown, there were no rats and no dead fish. Yet just a year earlier, during the summer of 1940, a "Puffs and Pot Shots" column in the *Advocate* asked, "Are the supporters of cleaner beaches asleep?" Next to the Portuguese Bakery on Commercial Street, writer Irving S. Rogers noted on July 11, 1940, that a "recently installed sewerage line to the shore" was weighted down with rocks. "The sewer is practically under the Board of Trade windows, and the loudest clamor about cleaner beaches originates in this building."

Rogers, who also served as chairman of the board of health, led a major beach cleanup in June 1941, prior to Nin's arrival. That cleanup brought in such a loathsome collection of broken-down items, including toilet bowls, rusty oil drums and even girdles—113 loads—that one wondered how anyone could swim in such a dirty place. Furthermore, it had been the practice for many decades to dump kitchen garbage out on the beach and let the tides carry most of it away. Tourists, in particular, sometimes commented on the odor this practice created. Residents were, apparently, immune.

In May 1942, longtime summer visitor Dudley R. Wood of Livingston, New Jersey, wrote to the *Advocate* that while he and his wife loved the shoreline, "the lovely vistas lose their charm when accompanied by mounds of garbage and offal with their attendant stench."

Wood noted that disease would "attack the innocent summer visitor" as quickly as it attacked the malefactor who was tossing the offal onto the beach.

"We are not more than ordinarily squeamish, I think, but we honestly begin to fear those festering piles of putrefaction, which were permitted to gather and rot under the simmering heat of the summer sun," he continued. One can only imagine the flies, maggots and rats that gleefully gathered in such a place.

Wood contributed two dollars toward the beach cleanup fund. For the immediate future, beach cleanups were annual events.

Bombs Over Pearl Harbor, the Monument Goes Dark

On December 7, 1941, everything changed in America.

On December 7, the Japanese attacked Pearl Harbor. The next day, in a speech in which President Franklin D. Roosevelt declared the day "a date which will live in infamy," Roosevelt asked Congress for a declaration of war. All of a sudden, in an unseasonably warm New England December, men were enlisting or being drafted. And would the Japanese send in more bombers? If so, what would they target? For those living along the coasts, or out in the Atlantic on the "sandy fist" of what Thoreau dubbed Massachusetts's "bared and bended arm," Cape Cod, it was terrifying.

The Pilgrim Monument was the first building to go dark. Previously, it had been illuminated "from base to top with strong flood lights, [and] by night it stood a mighty and gleaming shaft that could be seen many miles away," the *Advocate* reported. Now it was lit by only a red light on top to guide airplanes. There would also be no Christmas lights along the streets.

Civilian defense teams were immediately organized, and one of their first tasks was to visit the town's houses and list everyone, particularly the invalids and aged.

Chief air raid warden H. Clinton Owen called for nearly two hundred citizens to enlist as air raid wardens. No time was wasted, and a couple

The Pilgrim Monument was the first building to go dark under wartime regulations in 1941. *Collection of the author.*

of days after the raid at Pearl Harbor, over seventy-five American legionnaires agreed to assume active duty at a "cold, unfriendly and dismal spot" at the watch post on Beach Point. *Advocate* writer Irving Rogers and Maurice Nevins took the first watch as spotters.

Armed with sandwiches and a jug of oil for the stove "to keep our teeth from chattering," Rogers and Nevins headed out to Beach Point on a windy and cold night. When the two men stumbling out to the watch shelter briefly switched on a flashlight, "heavy Navy searchlights" from the water "centered on us for a thorough investigation." Four destroyers and a submarine were anchored in the harbor, continuously on watch.

The moon rose over the dunes at 9:55 p.m., increasing visibility. "Once or twice a shooting star gave us an instant of alarm and we tried to figure out all lights that seemed at all strange." The three hours passed quickly, and the two watchers turned the post over to another pair. "However, there are many long and cold nights ahead but we all seem agreed that nothing will prevent our carrying on," Rogers said.[16]

Through a series of lectures, air raid wardens were trained in crowd control should bombs fall on Provincetown. An "expert gas man" came from Camp Edwards to describe various types of poisonous gases that might be encountered.[17] The air raid wardens also facilitated a graduated warning system: yellow, blue, red (imminent attack) and then white (all clear). Terms such as sodium bomb, thermite bomb and phosphorous "calling cards" suddenly entered the general vocabulary.

Although residents went about their daily lives, an air of menace and tension hung over them. We might compare this atmosphere to the weeks after September 11, 2001, when security was tight and nerves taut. Citizens of Germany, Italy and Japan, ages fourteen and over, had to register at the post office, bringing with them an interpreter, if needed, and three photo IDs. It was said that even the painter Hans Hofmann, a German native who had been naturalized in 1941, came under suspicion because of his habit of heading off to the beach to paint his abstract works.[18]

In mid-June, a "nest" of submarines "not many miles off the Back Shore" sank an American freighter and passenger steamer and a British freighter, killing ninety-four men. "Folks down along Beach Point, in town and as far south as Eastham heard explosions and saw bright flares in the sky out to sea," the *Advocate* reported on June 25, 1942. When survivors and the wounded were brought to shore, Provincetown residents stepped up to care for them with medical help, food, dry clothes and beds.

In July, the *Advocate* published the following curious news item in the center of page one, under the words "A Sworn Statement":

> *All roads leading to Provincetown and all bridges over which those roads must pass (including the Canal bridges) are as free and clear for travel as they have ever been at any time.*
>
> *No part of Provincetown is or has been under martial law.*
>
> *Stories that the Atlantic seaboard shores are littered with bodies, covered with oil and that the water is polluted with oil…are fantastic rot, certainly as far as the entire Lower Cape is concerned.*

The announcement said that "artists are permitted to sketch and paint as always" and that bathing "can be enjoyed without restrictions of any kind." The piece was signed by Paul George Lambert, editor, and endorsed by N. Edwin Lewis, chairman of the board of selectmen. Most unusually, it was notarized on July 9. We can assume the newspaper and town fathers were reacting to bizarre rumors.

Artists might have been welcome in Provincetown, but could they come? The artist Sara Lois Wood, who had been a student of Arthur Diehl, a gifted showman artist who priced his dune paintings by the square inch, came to Provincetown every summer with her husband, photographer Jim O'Brien. The pair was "a Provincetown summer institution," known for selling Wood's work from their "motor caravan," which they used as their living quarters parked behind the Cape Codder Restaurant. But during the summer of 1942, O'Brien was an inspector in an Alcoa plant, and Wood was running a drill press for Sikorsky Aircraft in Connecticut. She told the *Advocate* that she was one of seven "girls" and fifty-odd men on the 6:30 p.m. to 4:00 a.m. shift. "I've had so many steel and aluminum splinters in my hands that I was becoming popular as a back scratcher," Wood joked. "I feel a little quakey inside when I look at my paint brushes, but I close my eyes quickly—and say, 'this won't last forever.'"

One person who did come to Provincetown during the summer of 1942 was Peggy Guggenheim, the wealthy art collector and gallery owner. Guggenheim was at that time married to her third husband, Max Ernst, a surrealist painter who was born in Germany and had already been interned in a camp in France. Ernst had come ahead to the Cape with Guggenheim's daughter and rented a house in Wellfleet. When Guggenheim arrived, she moved the family to Provincetown. This caused a debacle much like the one in March 1917, during World War I, when Eugene O'Neill was arrested on an espionage charge after he was caught walking in the dunes with what was probably a typewriter. In this case, because Ernst failed to register with the authorities as an enemy alien, he was questioned. His "cryptic answers," as well as the presence of a shortwave radio in the house where the family was staying, led to a suspicion of espionage. After a great deal of effort, Guggenheim got Ernst off the hook, and the pair returned to New York.[19] Guggenheim is more than a footnote to this story, as the following October she opened her Art of This Century Gallery in New York City; the gallery would represent Robert Motherwell. She also gave Hans Hofmann his first one-man show in 1944.

Motherwell had been in Mexico earlier in the year with the artist Roberto Matta, whose house Guggenheim's family was sharing. Motherwell had graduated from Stanford University in 1937, with a degree in philosophy, and continued on to Harvard for graduate work. Now, on August 16, Motherwell married the actress Maria Emilia Ferreira y Moyers, whom he had met in Mexico and who would be the first of his four wives. Motherwell recalled the war years in Provincetown as depressing ones.

"The claustrophobic silent dark of those World War II nights here remains with me like a black stone," he wrote. His lack of money surely colored his attitude, too. "I think we had $600 for the four-month summer. Going to the movies meant a tin of beans for supper."[20]

In early September, the air warden conducted a blackout drill that left Provincetown in darkness for thirty minutes from 9:55 to 10:25 p.m.

The abstract expressionist painter Robert Motherwell was associated with Provincetown for nearly fifty years. His signature appears on his 1991 headstone in Provincetown Cemetery. *Photo by the author.*

The only light came from the "rain-washed stars that sprinkled the night sky after the storm last night, a few fireflies going about their business oblivious of air raid wardens, and the long sweeps of Highland brushing the town with light."[21]

In December, the "72,000 eyes and ears" of Cape Codders were asked to detect signs of enemy activity. "Hyannis-10,000" was the phone number to call with reports of funny business such as "fires, signals, flares, suspicious landings, wreckage, flotsam, parachutes, submarines, mines and torpedoes." The residents of Cape Cod "want no German vermin using our sand dunes as spring boards to the productions heart of the allied world."

The following February, those under age sixteen were put under a 9:00 p.m. curfew. The police chief blew the fire whistle at 8:45 p.m. "as the curfew signal." Voters at the town meeting in February approved the expenditure of $1,000 for training citizens in first aid. Meanwhile, $500 was put toward the Eastern School Building, which was used as a recreation center for the many soldiers and sailors swarming through town.

Rationing Brings Quiet Summers

As the war years continued, every aspect of life was touched. The 661 students enrolled in the Provincetown schools took part in the war effort. One group collected eight tons of newspapers. The schoolchildren in Governor Bradford School collected enough scrap metal in the spring of 1943 to almost fill the town's quota.

The war filtered into the school curriculum, too. Physical education classes were designed to prepare boys for the army. "The youngster who is embarrassed in physical education classes about dressing and undressing in front of others may be shocked by barracks life, unless guidance prepares him," a school official wrote in the 1943 *Town Records and Reports*. That year, during routine school physicals, "the feet are, at present, being examined somewhat more carefully than usual at request of the state," wrote A.P. Goff, MD, the county health officer.

The girls were not left out. In the bookkeeping section of the commercial course, the section on groceries was revised to include instruction on shopping on a complicated ration system.

Rationing must have been one of the dreariest aspects of the war.

It began with tires at the end of December 1941. "Today's doughboy rolls on rubber," the *Advocate* announced in January, which meant that the folks back home rolled on their rims. Selectman Jesse D. Rogers announced that a committee of three would oversee tire rationing. For the month of January, the entire town of Provincetown was allocated two passenger or motorcycle tires and tubes, nine truck tires and seven tubes. (That number decreased in February.) The town's doctors, Thomas Perry and Daniel H. Hiebert, were allocated tires. They must have gotten one each.

By the spring, rumors were rife that gasoline would soon be rationed, and for Provincetown, this meant more than an annoyance—it meant that the summer tourist trade might go under. By some estimates, 60 percent of the town's income came from the summer business.[22]

"It seems that the hard working city folks feel that 'we are going away for a vacation this year if we have to walk, crawl or creep,'" Irving Rogers wrote in his "Puffs and Pot Shots" column on March 26. In fact, the rosy Rogers saw some benefit to the town being nearly car-free. "Maybe in prowling around these narrow streets they will be able to put a finger on some of the things that have been drawing them here from year to year."

Heinrich Pfeiffer, who ran a summer theater, also predicted a great summer—albeit a quieter one than usual. Because the Boston day boat

Provincetown High School students helped with the war effort. The final senior class of eight graduated in 2013; the school was converted for the use of students through the eighth grade. *Photo by the author.*

would not be running, tourists would have to arrive on buses. Pfeiffer thought this would be a plus, as the town would be "freed, for once, after a long time, of its honky-tonk." By "honky-tonk," he meant a certain type of day-tripper—the type who stumbled off the boat, ate a meal, bought a few souvenirs and then reboarded for the return trip to Boston.

Yet even Pfeiffer admitted that his summer theater was up in the air because it was difficult to find male actors and he'd have to settle for the few whom "Uncle Sam doesn't insist on taking."

Pfeiffer's optimism, however, could not quell townsfolk's fears, especially when it was learned that stringent gasoline rationing would begin on May 15. Most people would be limited to two and a half gallons of gas a week.

Late in April, sugar was the first commodity to be rationed, and sugar books, each containing twenty-eight stamps, were distributed. One pound of sugar was given out every two weeks with a stamp.

Each time something new was rationed, ration cards had to be distributed to the entire population. School superintendent Alton E. Ramey was in charge of handing out gas ration cards. This system was made complicated in that certain privileged individuals were given what were known as X ration cards. X card holders could have unlimited gasoline. The thirty-one X cards in Provincetown were given to doctors, for example, and other crucial personnel.

"There were 'gas chiselers' here as elsewhere, about ten percent," Ramey estimated in the April 30, 1942 *Advocate*. Chiselers "were out to get all the gas they could by hook or by crook."

Just before rationing took effect, there was a run on gas stations with patrons and gas monkeys alike saying, "Fill 'er up"—words that would not be heard again until the end of the war.

The Summer of '42

And then all at once, the summer of '42, the first wartime summer, was in full swing. "There are no noisy and madcap steamboat crowds to get in your hair," the *Advocate* crowed. Traffic was just right on the streets—parking was ample. People employed "foot-work and bicycles to prowl about the town." And the town crier was silent.

As far as the Fourth of July went, if you could get yourself to Provincetown, ten or so local gas stations had plenty of gas—for those with coupons.

The SS *Steel Pier*, which brought day-trippers from Boston and gave them a few hours to eat lunch and see artists in their natural habitat, ceased running during the war. *Collection of the author.*

The Flagship's block ad of July 16, 1942 reflected the times:

No Dim-Out of Activity
No Black-Out of Entertainment
No Rationing of Hospitality
No Priorities of Pleasure.
At the Flagship.

Visitor Denis Plimmer moaned in an *Advocate* letter to the editor on July 30, 1942, that "times are bad in P'town this year of our Lord, 1942." But he went on to say that while the stress and deprivations of war had made folks surly and nasty in New York, everyone in Provincetown, in contrast, was friendly and helpful.

Rubber boots were rationed in October. On the other hand, coffee and bacon, which were not rationed, were impossible to come by. So maybe things were looking up when coffee was rationed in mid-November. Those under the age of fourteen, hooked on caffeine or not, would not be given ration stamps for coffee. Those fourteen and over had a chance of obtaining it. Late in October, heating fuel, too, was rationed, which meant a chilly winter ahead for many, including the Provincetown Library, which was then in a house at 330 Commercial Street. Because kerosene was rationed, the first floor could not be heated above sixty degrees. The second-floor reading room was closed altogether, and the librarian on duty ran upstairs every so often in her overcoat to fetch books requested by patrons.

The War Drags On and Garbage Piles Up

By now, as the war was about to enter its second full summer, there was little talk of the upcoming summer season. "And maybe that's going to be good for Provincetown—awfully good," the *Advocate* suggested. "Maybe we need to think about Provincetown as an all-year round town and not as a ten-week, hell-raisin', summertime, holiday place."

Life was tough with the bulk of the hale and hearty male population away. One week during the summer, rubbish was not picked up; other times, it was picked up a day or two later than usual. Why was this? The labor shortage.

"By night Provincetown was blacked-out, and by day the streets were bare of automobiles, except for local machines of limited fuel allowance," wrote the artist Ross Moffatt in his book *Art in Narrow Streets*, describing the summer of 1943. "Missing from the town were nearly all civilians of military age."

"The year 1943 has been a sad one, for many of our young people have entered the Service," wrote librarian Penelope V. Kern in the 1943 *Town Records and Reports*. "Words cannot say how much we miss them and how anxious we feel for their welfare." The following February, Jesse A. Silva was killed, earning the distinction of being Provincetown's first serviceman killed at the battlefront. The twenty-seven-year-old was also the town's only paratrooper. A resident of Bradford Street, he had attended Provincetown High and worked at the Cape Cod Cold Storage before he enlisted. A square is named after him at the corner of Howland and Bradford Streets.

Williams Returns to Eat More Fish

The summer of '44 was much like the previous two wartime summers. With recreation restricted, a record number of summer people took to reading library books.

Tennessee Williams, whose draft status was IV-F because of a serious cataract problem in his left eye, returned to Provincetown to celebrate the Fourth of July, this time checking into "a little shanty

During the Hurricane of 1944, MIT scientists manned a weather station at Race Point. The 1897 Old Harbor Life-Saving Station was moved to Race Point from Chatham in 1977. *Photo by Deane Folsom II.*

in the dunes where I can avoid the summer crowd." He was economizing by eating fish again, and he planned to remain in Provincetown for a while because it was cheaper than New York. "Practically the entire lunatic fringe of Manhattan are among the summer colonists at P-town," he wrote to Jay Laughlin in late July.[23]

It seems cruel when people are already laboring under difficult wartime circumstances that Mother Nature should pile on something terrible. So it was with the awesome Hurricane of 1944, which made the Hurricane of 1938 "seem like a pleasant zephyr," as the *Advocate* noted on September 28, 1944.

Unlike in 1938, in 1944, residents were given fair warning and time to prepare for the storm. The Coast Guard called in its men. Fishing boats were tied up to moorings, and any remaining pleasure boats were tied to double sea anchors. Naval vessels departed for the relative safety of the Cape Cod Canal. "For two days now there has been a feeling of ominous

foreboding in Provincetown," the *Advocate* said on September 14, 1944. The thirteenth was "dank, heavy and sultry and so very, very quiet." At 5:00 p.m., fog rolled in. The shoreline was carpeted with "bright green sea growth churned up by a nor'easter," and in the air was the odor of "dead clam flats." By mid-morning, two square red flags were flying on the top of the staff on Monument Hill. That was a hurricane warning.

MIT scientists were out at Race Point at the government experimental station, preparing their weather equipment. As they did so, they were harassed by a skunk with its head stuck in a pickle bottle. "Everywhere the men turned to batten down for the storm and set up their hurricane equipment, there was that skunk, tilting up the pickle bottle to watch the excitement."[24]

Sales of liquor ended at 6:00 p.m., and a curfew was on at 9:00 p.m. as the town battened down.

The town went dark at 11:11 p.m.; wind gusts reached their peak of one hundred miles per hour at 12:08 a.m. "Throughout its howling could be heard the crashing of glass, the thud of falling bricks and the tearing of branches." The rain was "driving like bullets."[25]

At last, about 2:30 a.m., the rain stopped and the winds diminished to fifty-seven miles per hour. The skunk at Race Point wandered away as the storm abated. At daybreak, scenes on Commercial Street were "sickening." Branches were lying in the streets amid tangles of wires and glass from broken windows. The chimney at the library had plunged through the building's high mansard roof. Entire streets were blocked by venerable elms that had tumbled in the darkness. Of thirty-two fish traps owned by Atlantic Coast Fisheries, only two remained. Many fishing boats were also destroyed.

Telephone and telegraph contact was down. Just as had happened after the Hurricane of 1938, newspaper reports of the destruction were wildly exaggerated. The *Advocate* noted, on September 21, 1944, that the *Boston Post* reported that "Cape Tip Is Left in Ruins." The *Post* article went on to magnify the destruction and reported that Provincetown was under martial law with the town "unrecognizable." Unable to verify the reports, some friends and family of Provincetown residents "piled provisions into their cars to battle their way to Provincetown and nourish those still alive."

Gert's Garbage

"In some ways Provincetown is like Times Square in New York," wrote a columnist in the *Advocate* the following spring, in April 1945. "Sooner or later everyone will visit both places, and most people have been here at some time or other."

As the war in Europe entered its final months, Valeska Gert for one, was in Provincetown, running a nightclub on the water named Valeska's.

Born Gertrud Valeska Samosch on January 11, 1892, in Berlin, Valeska Gert, or simply Gert, as she was generally known, began dance lessons at age nine and became an avant-garde stage and silent film performer. In 1929, she played the headmistress of a reform school in *Diary of a Lost Girl* starring Louise Brooks. When the Nazis banned her from performing on account of her Jewish heritage, she emigrated in 1938 and ended up in New York, where she ran a bar-cabaret called Beggar's Bar in the Village. Tennessee Williams worked for her at the end of 1941—as a waiter. According to Williams's *Memoir*, Williams was paid solely in tips. To increase those tips, he began reciting his "pretty raw" verse until he "became something of a draw" and received sizable tips. When Gert announced the waiters would pool their tips and split them with management (Gert herself), Williams balked. An abstract painter who happened to be present took Williams's side and hurled soda bottles at Gert. That mêlée ended Williams's career as a waiter.

Gert had performed in Provincetown in the summer of 1941 at the White Whale & Mooring Mast on Sunday nights. As one reviewer in the *Advocate* remarked, "The young lady's singing antics are said to well-nigh put her in the acrobatic class." As Gert was then nearly fifty, her act must have been convincing in many ways.

By 1945, Gert was running her own place, Valeska's at 355 Commercial Street, where she served "international food" from 6:00 p.m. with "entertainment" beginning at 9:00 p.m. and including "Two Blitz Shows Nightly at 10 and 11 P.M." Entertainers were Gert, Maria Collm and a Madame Pumpernickel, who was said to be a seventy-year-old piano-playing midget. Late night snacks were served until 1:00 a.m.[26]

"Stop, Thief!"

Something odd was in the air during that final summer of the war. On July 5, 1945, a letter from the forty-one-year-old writer Raube Walters of Brookline was printed in the *Advocate*. Walters, like Williams before him, took a studio at Captain Jack's Wharf. Accompanied by his Irish terrier, he worked in longhand on a manuscript, "piling up page after page in folders until five chapters were finished. I was happy and enamored of Provincetown." On the night of Wednesday, June 27, Walters went out to dinner "feeling very much at peace with the world." When he returned from dinner, however, he found he had been robbed of an unusual collection of items: a clock, some pipes, socks, handkerchiefs, the dog's leash and the manuscript. The police later chalked up the incident to "irresponsible boys." Walters, however, claimed it was the responsibility of the entire community to create *responsible* boys.

Walters is best known today for his 1931 novel, *The Hex Woman*, about three sisters forced into witchcraft in Pennsylvania Dutch country.

And then, on the night of August 8, as the war in Europe wound down, a bizarre attack occurred at Valeska's with "a barrage of missiles hurled into the place from the bay side," a Mrs. Lillian DaCosta of Bradford Street complained in a letter to the editor. Calling it "a disgraceful and dangerous exhibition of hoodlumism which shocked us," DaCosta compared it to "the sort of thing that might have happened in Nazi Germany."

Although it remains unclear whether the "missiles" were trash or some sort of projectiles, this was, in fact, the sort of incident that Gert had left Berlin to escape.

Now, the question might be this: was this "barrage of missiles" related to Gert's upcoming appearance in the Second District Court the following morning? It seemed that many neighbors had observed Gert dumping her trash on the beach. The artist Julius Katzieff and a friend of his, O.F. McIntyre, had spied Gert empty "half a barrel of trash and garbage" on the beach under the cover of darkness at 1:00 a.m. on August 6—no doubt right after her final "late snacks" were cleared away. This might not have been so bad if Gert had not already been warned about dumping garbage and was already looking down the barrel at a $100 fine. Gert's defense? She said she didn't know where to put the garbage.

Bizarre though Gert's words might sound to us now, as we have seen, dumping garbage on the beach, particularly in the center of town along Commercial Street, was a centuries-old practice, only recently halted.

But now the town had a dump, and in some parts of town, trash was picked up, albeit irregularly. Garbage pickups were discontinued after Labor Day. Because people were moving back to their winter quarters at that time, and leaving their trash at curbside, the rubbish sometimes sat on the curb for two weeks. Despite all of these provisos and a history of dumping anywhere, Judge Robert A. Welsh, whose court was sitting in Provincetown Town Hall, felt Gert had no excuse.

"Judge Welsh used this first example of garbage-throwing on the beach to be brought before him as an occasion to state the views of the court on a practice which is common in certain sections of the shore, particularly in the central business section," the *Advocate* reported on August 9, 1945. While sections of the shore at each end of town were "as fine as any to be found anywhere," parts of the central shore "were about as bad as the worst in the world."

Welsh gave Gert a week to pay her $100 fine, but Gert's day in court was not over. Madame Pumpernickel, also known as Helen Hawks, had brought a civil suit for back wages against Gert. By the end the day, Gert was out of pocket an additional $42 in back wages and court costs.

The War Ends with a Bang

By the time Gert appeared in court, World War II had only another five days to run before the armistice. It had been a long war.

"For days Provincetown had been sitting with its ear to the radio, hopes rising, hopes falling, trying to sort out something sound in all the rumors of peace, surrender and victory," the *Advocate* reported on August 16, 1945. "But then it came. Then it really came. And Provincetown man, woman and child, picked itself up by the pants, bootstraps and halter and hurled itself into the wildest, gayest celebration this town has ever known."

Car horns blared, fire sirens rang, freezer whistles blew and people "tumbled" out to the streets, cheering in a blaze of confetti. It was a moment of the "delirium of joy."

After he was demobilized, Robert Harrison, whose home was at that time in Boston, came down to Provincetown. Harrison had spent the war as an ensign in the U.S. Navy on a destroyer escort in the Pacific that was searching for Japanese submarines. Harrison was familiar with the town from boyhood vacations—his parents, particularly his mother, loved it. Yet even Harrison,

A carnival-like atmosphere has prevailed in summertime Provincetown for decades. Here David "Scarbie" Mitchell advertises *Lip-Schtick*, his "one-person" show featuring "nine personalities," in July 2011. *Photo by Carolyn Brault Seefer.*

who eventually adopted Provincetown as his home and stayed for over fifty years, found the immediate postwar atmosphere too wild.

"It was like a coiled spring that sprung," he said.[27] "All these people who had come back—it was completely crazy. Drag queens with the tops open, make-up and all that kind of thing—anything goes," he recalled. "It didn't last long but that was what went on. Clothes, actions, language—it was mad. I didn't like it.

"I looked around Commercial Street and I said, 'This is not for me.'"

Harrison returned to Harvard and finished his degree. A few years later, when things were tamer, he returned to Provincetown and, with his partner Harold Goodstein, established the hotel Hargood House on the East End of Commercial Street. But over six decades later, he still remembered that wild summer after the war.

"Push and Pull"

In 1945, the famous abstract expressionist painter and art teacher Hans Hofmann bought Frederick Waugh's house and studio at 76 Commercial Street, the place with which he would be most strongly associated.

Hofmann, born in 1880 and a refugee from Europe, was one of the most influential summer residents of Provincetown for decades. Hofmann had studied in Paris from 1904 to 1914, and "the importance of what he learned there cannot be overestimated."[28] The art critic Irving Sandler has called those heady years "the heroic decade of twentieth-century art," a time when various schools of art such as cubism, fauvism, futurism and German expressionism were all in play.[29]

Hawthorne, who had established Provincetown's art colony in 1899, had died in 1930, leaving a gap in art instruction in Provincetown. (That was the same year fifty-year-old Hofmann emigrated from Germany.) In 1935, Hofmann opened a summer art school in Hawthorne's old studio on Miller Hill Road while teaching in New York City for the rest of the year.

To Hofmann's students, every word was gold—even though the students might not have understood the deaf Hofmann's thick German accent. His English was studded with *nicht wahr*, and as Motherwell said, "because he was difficult to understand, you couldn't doubt or challenge him."[30] Hofmann taught a "push and pull" mantra of composition, which he illustrated with a description of a balloon. When you press one side, "push answers with pull, and pull with push."[31] Hofmann critiqued his students sometimes by ripping their drawings into four pieces, which he rearranged, or even drawing over their compositions. On Friday afternoons, "artists and other visitors from all over the Cape congregated" to watch Hofmann's "theatrical" critiques.[32]

Lee Krasner, who later married Jackson Pollock, enrolled in Hofmann's school on West Ninth Street in New York and followed him to Provincetown

"The minute you entered that house, you were enveloped in a wave of affection," art curator Katharine Kuh wrote about Hans and Miz Hofmann's house at 76 Commercial Street. *Photo by the author.*

for further instruction in the summers. Like others, she found she couldn't understand Hofmann's English for a good six months. On Krasner's first Friday "crit," Hofmann tore the lower part of her painting into pieces and reassembled them "to achieve greater dynamism."[33] Sandler, who was a young man working menial jobs such as washing floors at Ciro & Sal's during the summers of 1955 to 1958, recalls sneaking in to Hofmann's Friday critiques. "His eye was always on color, how to make it luminous and keep it from being 'mono-tone-eous,'" Sandler wrote.

Among Hofmann's many, many students were Louise Nevelson, Red Grooms, Helen Frankenthaler and pop artist Larry Rivers.

Artists fondly recalled visiting the hospitable Hofmann and his wife, Miz, who had finally joined her husband after leaving Munich in 1939. "Everything about Hans was welcoming," the art curator Katharine Kuh remembered. "The minute you entered that house, you were enveloped in a wave of affection."[34]

While Hofmann is primarily honored as a teacher, he also painted, dressed in baggy pants and a short-sleeved shirt—if not nude—while listening to Bach. His palette was a thirty- by forty-inch sheet of glass; cadmium and cobalt blues were his favorite shades. He applied paint so thickly to his canvases that it sometimes took up to two years for the resulting impasto to dry. The results were paintings such as *Terpsichore*, colorful fusions of abstract expressionism and cubism. His paintings were "a challenging and original abstract style rooted firmly in the visible world."[35] Hofmann loved the water, and seascapes and aquatic themes were said to fascinate him.

"In many of Hofmann's paintings done in Provincetown, I find, or perhaps I imagine I find, the changing moods of the sea," Kuh wrote. "That shining expanse of water immediately across from his house must have affected his sensibilities."

What Is Provincetown without Its Town Crier?

On the Fourth of July 1947, a passenger off the Boston boat tried to nab a souvenir from town crier Amos Kubik, who was decked out in a Pilgrim costume. It was the crier's habit to greet the ferry when it pulled in, standing on the wharf "crying" about various restaurants where the mobs from the boat might eat lunch.

When George E. Seely of Newtonville stepped off the gangplank, he made a beeline for the crier, first attempting to snatch his belt and then the buckles from his shoes. After a ruckus, Seely was arrested and eventually brought before Judge Robert A. Welsh.[36] Seely told the judge he was an insurance salesman who collected antiques. The judge responded that the crier was "an institution" and added, "Apparently you thought he was an antique." In his defense, Seely claimed he had gone into the boat's washroom to shave, and while in there, a stranger had pressed two drinks, presumably alcoholic or laced with drugs, on him. That was the last thing he remembered until he woke up in the police station. Seely was found guilty of rude and disorderly conduct and drunkenness. He was fined ten dollars.[37]

Provincetown, like many New England towns, had long used town criers to spread news rapidly in those days before radio and television. Town crier George Washington Ready gained long-lasting fame in 1886 when he claimed he spotted an immense sea serpent half a mile from the shore in Herring Cove. In his more usual work as town crier, Ready walked up Commercial Street ringing his brass bell and shouting "Notice!" Even after he retired and turned his bell over to Walter T. "Hoppy" Smith, tourists still sought out Ready to hear his sea serpent story firsthand.

Town crier Walter L. Smith carried a notebook and bell. The crier once served an important role in disseminating news; later, he played to the tourist trade. *Collection of the author.*

Smith also served the function of classified advertising. The *New York Times* reported in 1916 that for one dollar, Smith would shout out the details of the item you were hawking. Smith, as it turned out, "was the last of the non-theatrical criers."[38] He hung up his bell in 1930.

The position of town crier was dropped for a few years until the owner of the Provincetown Inn decided to hire Kubik, a native of Bohemia with an intense interest in American history, to cry privately to advertise the hotel. The innkeeper decked Kubik out in a gold Pilgrim costume. Eventually, the town officially revived the profession. During the 1930s, tourists photographed the crier incessantly, and "children trail him."[39]

For a time, Frank Andrews, age seventy-four, a character actor from New York, took over the position of town crier. Decked out in a maroon Pilgrim costume, Andrews proclaimed his "only discomfort" was "weary dogs," referring to his size-eleven feet. As it turned out, Andrews served as town crier for only one season and was replaced by actor Charles Walton the following summer.

During the first war summer of 1942, when the boat from Boston no longer made its daily run to Provincetown, the town crier, too, was discontinued. "His office was merely commercial and theatrical," sniffed the *New York Times*.

Yet Kubik turned up again in August 1945, dressed in full town crier outfit, on the cover of *Telephone Topics* magazine, seated at Provincetown's switchboard and wearing a telephone operator's head set. The photo was supposed to send a message about communication systems old and new, but it also sent a message about gender bending, particularly as the *Advocate* referred to Kubik as the "beautiful girl" on the cover.[40]

Throughout the twentieth century, the town boasted a crier off and on, as he was rightly valued as a draw for tourists and for his ability to shunt tourists into various restaurants and galleries. And it appears that Pilgrim costumes came in all sorts of colors. In 1962, town crier Arthur P. Snader, decked out in a blue costume, graced the cover of the *Town Records and Reports*. That year, the town budgeted $750 in "personal services" and another $100 for expenses for the town crier.

A Streetcar in the Atomic Age

In 1947, Tennessee Williams again returned to Cape Cod and rented a "shingled bungalow directly on the water somewhere between North Truro and Provincetown." He shared the bungalow with several others, and at some point both the plumbing and the electricity fizzled out. Williams divided his time between mornings at the typewriter and afternoons in the sunny dunes beyond Provincetown. One evening when he went to the Atlantic House to hear Stella Brooks, the jazz singer, he met Frank Merlo, who was to become his companion of the next several years.[41] Today, a nude photo of Williams walking on the beach hangs in one of the bars at the Atlantic House.

The Atlantic House, or A-House, as it is now known, was built in 1798 on Masonic Place and boasts that it became a "gay-friendly" establishment in the 1950s, when Reggie Cabral, its late owner/manager, took over. In the summer of 1955, Billie Holiday, Eartha Kitt and Ella Fitzgerald all sang at the A-House. Today, the A-House is owned by Cabral's daughter April Cabral-Pitzner and boasts three bars: the Dance Club, with its Friday night theme parties; the Little Bar, a year-round gathering spot with its fireplace; and the Macho Bar, a leather bar.

It was that summer, in that bungalow, as the story goes, when Marlon Brando arrived to audition for the role of Stanley Kowalski in *A Streetcar Named Desire* and ended up fixing both the plumbing and electricity.[42]

That summer, the theme of the Artists' Ball, sponsored by the Provincetown Arts Association, was "The Atomic Age." A prize was given for the best costume—"Bikini," worn by Mrs. Warren Holmes. Holmes's multicolored hat represented the "now familiar billows of smoke that are created by the explosion of the mighty bomb." Harry Kemp, variously

This gorgeous circa 1830 West End house was home to the family of Reggie Cabral (1924–1996), owner of the famous long-running nightclub the A-House. *Photo by Deane Folsom II.*

known as the "tramp poet" or the "dune poet," attended the ball robed in "conventional poet's garb with evergreen headdress and carried signs decrying the atomic bomb."

Death of Playwright Susan Glaspell

As those of the earlier generation who founded the Provincetown Players died off, reminders of mortality were given to those left behind. Susan Glaspell died on July 27, 1948, at the age of sixty-six at her home at 564 Commercial Street. At one time, according to her obituary in the *New York Times*, she "was one of the nation's most widely read novelists." Her husband was the classicist George Cram Cook; Glaspell, Cook and their friends founded the Provincetown Players. Glaspell herself had won a Pulitzer Prize in 1931 for her feminist play *Alison's House*. She had lived in Provincetown since 1912.

Edmund Wilson, a longtime friend of Glaspell, had once rented her Commercial Street house while she was living in Truro. Wilson attended Glaspell's funeral early on the afternoon of July 28 and, in a letter to his wife, Elena, called the service "dismal." It "depressed me with the thought of how little there was left of the original idealism and enthusiasm of the old P-town group."[43]

In his diary, he wrote, "I felt, as I had not done before, that we...had all become a group, a community, more closely bound up together than we had realized or perhaps wanted to be." He went on to recall parties, trips to the beach, picnics, flirtations, drinking and work. "Pictures and figures by local artists accumulated in P'town front rooms, walled in against the street—that was what our life had been when we had dedicated ourselves to the Cape, to the life of the silver harbor."[44]

"Hail, Thou Star of Ocean"

The Captains Association proposed a blessing of the fleet event such as the one held annually in the fishing town of Gloucester, north of Boston. So it was that the first blessing took place on June 27, 1948. With the town gaily decorated with bunting, the morning began with the fishermen "arrayed in their Sunday best" and assembled in front of the Knights of Columbus Hall. Accompanied by the Santo Christo band, the group marched to the Church of St. Peter the Apostle, where a high mass was celebrated. At 2:45 p.m., the group reassembled and, accompanied by the Most Reverend James E. Cassidy, bishop of Fall River, gathered at the wharf under the gaze of the entire town and hundreds of visitors.[45]

"Finally Provincetown's crew of rugged fishermen appeared in a procession through the crowd, no longer arrayed in their Sunday best, but in their more favored working woolens of vivid colors and shouting checks," the *Advocate* reported. Cassidy said he was honored the Lord chose "St. Peter, a fisherman, as the leader and founder of the church." He then went on to say he had been shipwrecked no fewer than three times and saved each time because he knew how to swim. He exhorted Provincetown's parents to teach their kids to swim—advice that earned him high praise in the *Advocate*. The service ended with everyone singing "Hail, Thou Star of Ocean." The fishermen then got on their boats and made an arc out to Long Point and back, "passing within a few feet of

The first blessing of the fleet took place in 1948; it has become an annual tradition in June. Sadly, in recent years, Provincetown's fishing fleet has been reduced in size. *Photo by Deane Folsom II.*

where the Bishop stood, each boat to receive his special blessing." By the end of the summer, a group of boat owners, captains and members of the Seafood Producers Association had agreed to make the blessing of the fleet an annual event.

The summer of 1948 was perhaps quieter than the immediate postwar summers had been. The poet Weldon Kees, who organized Forum 49 the following summer, reported to a friend on July 22, "Provincetown seems less crowded than during other seasons I've been up here." Many "regulars" are away, Kees wrote, and the merchants complain about business. "Most of the night clubs are deserted: and from the quality of their entertainers, well deserve to be."[46]

Yet a grotesque incident a few days later reminds us that the 1940s were a harsh decade. Someone set up an inflated rubber raft in front of town hall, and in it, "more dead than alive," was an alligator billed at three hundred pounds. A banner hanging nearby depicted a gladiator wrestling with the alligator. Adding to the carnival atmosphere, a truck equipped with a megaphone drove through town promoting a wrestling match set to occur that evening between the alligator and a man.

"It is this kind of thing that will keep substantial people away from Provincetown except when they want to go slumming," the *Advocate* ranted on August 5. "We have hit a new low."

Forum 49

Kees, born in 1914, died so mysteriously that some doubted that he was, in fact, dead. His car was found on July 19, 1955, near the Golden Gate Bridge in San Francisco. Although his body was never recovered, there was no doubt that Kees was gone, and it was assumed that he jumped from the bridge and drowned.

In the late 1940s, Kees had taken up painting, and in 1948, he and his wife, Ann, began summering in Provincetown while wintering in California. In the summer of 1949, fifty years after Charles Webster Hawthorne arrived in Provincetown, Kees organized a summer-long series of panel discussions

The Julie Heller East Gallery, which bills itself as the oldest gallery in town, specializes in Provincetown's landmark artists. The Julie Heller East Gallery is at 465 Commercial Street. *Photo by the author.*

and exhibits. The venue was Donald F. Witherstine's 200 Gallery at 200 Commercial Street. The show paid homage to abstract expressionism and featured works by Hans Hofmann, Jackson Pollock and Robert Motherwell, among others.

In the photograph of Forum 1949, a white-haired woman who looks like everyone's great-aunt is seated alone in the front row. This is seventy-one-year-old "American Cubist" Blanche Lazzell (1878–1956). A pioneer of the American modernist movement, in 1918, Lazzell was among the founders of the Provincetown Printers Group, which created a style of woodblock print using a white-line method. In 1927, she was at the center of the passionate rift between the "Moderns" and the "Conservatives." And at age sixty, nearly deaf, she studied with Hofmann.

Forum 49 opened in July with an exhibition of "vanguard" abstract paintings by Lazzell, Ambrose E. Webster, Oliver Chaffee and Agnes Weinrich, a student of Hawthorne. That evening, four artists, including Hofmann, kicked off a ten-week series of lectures. The title of this one? "What Is an Artist?" It turned out that twice as many as could fit into the auditorium showed up in sweltering heat to hear the talk.

When it was Hofmann's turn to speak, he admitted that he didn't know what an artist was. He then "soberly listed the qualities an artist must have—creative instinct, a searching mind and fortitude," the *Advocate* reported on July 7, 1949.

In a way, this important postwar event set the stage for the next two decades, when Provincetown's galleries offered as sophisticated a group of paintings as might be found in New York City itself.

2
The Witch-Hunt Decade, 1950-1959

What I recall most strongly is the awareness of potential, of promise, of the clear and present possibility of future greatness.
—Art critic Irving Sandler on the 1950s in Provincetown

The Provincetown Witch Hunts

In 1940, before the war, the selectmen had spoken jeeringly of "darling men" after the summer season ended. That was only a preview of the searing homophobia to come in the 1950s.

"I give Provincetown three summers more, by which happy time the queers & their followers will have taken over (a few particularly vigorously bull lesbians perhaps tolerated & allowed to remain) and the last of the artistes looking with interest at Red Hook or the East Side of Brooklyn as new and promising sites for colonies," Weldon Kees wrote in a letter in the summer of 1951.[47]

The success of a tourist town depends, to some extent, on how well the town projects an image of itself to the wider world. In the case of Provincetown, the official image was that of an artsy, fun-loving, anything goes kind of place. It was just that some people didn't want the fun to have gay overtones. Ironically, through their efforts to suppress factions within the community, Provincetown's fathers managed to publicize aspects of the town that might not have been well known.

Homophobia is no longer tolerated in Provincetown. Today, Provincetown is billed as the "ultimate gay and lesbian vacation destination." *Photo by Deane Folsom II.*

In Provincetown, "these were the witch hunt days," retired Provincetown hotelier Robert Harrison said.

Town fathers have always had one tried and true item in their arsenal: deny liquor and entertainment licenses to those who offend their morals. In early June 1952, the selectmen tightened liquor and entertainment licenses to prohibit clubs from condoning obscene language, including in song, "so-called female impersonators" or an atmosphere encouraging "the habitual gathering place for homo-sexuals of either sex." The selectmen also disliked female bartenders. Any dancing would be out in the light, so that the genders of the dancers could be clearly seen.[48]

"That clean refreshing breeze drifting this way from Cape Cod undoubtedly is related to the fact that Provincetown has just slammed the door against an invasion of homosexuals," noted a *Boston Traveler* editorial reprinted in the *Advocate* on June 19, 1952. The editorial, under the headline "Provincetown Cleans House," dubbed homosexuals "drifters in the streets," "characters," "unwelcome migrants" and "undesirables" who turned the town into "an unsavory mess." The *Advocate* conceded that new licensing regulations had been met in town with "mixed reactions."

Six weeks later, on August 7, 1952, the paper printed an unsigned letter from a summer visitor who said that her two sons had been given doped cigarettes and then "powder to inhale" before they were taken to a place where "sex orgies followed." While she had now whisked her sons off to Europe for "a complete change and treatment," she wanted everyone to know that the daytime trysting spot was the beach in the dunes near the lighthouse and, at night, bars and apartments.

The selectmen sent out an inflammatory letter calling homosexuals "the lowest form of animal life." Incensing the board further was the fact that women running lodging houses "willingly house them" and "nightclub operators cater to them." The selectmen and police, on the other hand, intended to "rid our town of these degenerates." "Let us not permit our town to become a Sodom or Gomorrah," the letter concluded.

While the business community, led by Joseph E. Macara, president of the chamber of commerce, backed the police, saying that "Provincetown was committing suicide as a resort by condoning this disgusting situation," others saw it differently. In the August 14 *Advocate*, Jan Gelb, a painter, printmaker and art teacher, said some people were confusing "art with sodomy."

In 1949, Alice King and Al Jancik had opened a new club called Weathering Heights on Winthrop Street. The private club, where members paid dues, had a seasonal alcohol license and served a buffet dinner from 6:00 p.m. to midnight with entertainment and dancing. When the selectmen targeted the club at the end of the 1950s, they were obviously trying to put out of business a club that had a partly gay clientele.

One man who lived near the club's parking lot said he was sick and tired of hearing the "high-pitched voice and conversation of males on their way to a cocktail party at the club."

For years, it seemed that selectmen misunderstood their town's attractions. A Mrs. Earl Sylver wrote a letter to the editor on June 2, 1960, saying the town had been unfair to Weathering Heights. People are looking for something to do—they want to go out at night "where they can be entertained and relax." A week later, a "Mrs. Maddcap" wrote that all she saw at Weathering Heights was "a stout man singing songs and putting on one big beautiful hat after the other. I was surprised, because I had heard it was a spicy place to go." In other words, "Mrs. Maddcap" wanted to be titillated. Yet "all you see is nothing but hats and more hats."

This is, of course, a tongue-in-cheek reference to Weathering Heights's owner Phil Baiona, who took the stage name "Bayon." While doing his female impersonation act at Weathering Heights, he wore a huge "picture

Through the years, many vibrant nightspots have come and gone. The Governor Bradford Restaurant, which opened in 1960 at 312 Commercial Street, hosted a New Year's Eve Space Pussy party in 2013. *Photo by the author.*

hat"—a hat with a very wide brim—while being lowered from the ceiling on a swing.[49]

In July 1960, Weathering Heights finally lost its liquor license, and by August, Lucy Davidson, in her *Advocate* column "Items, Et cetera…" said that everyone was talking about the hearings held on Weathering Heights's license. "Tourists are aware of contention in the air." One couple she spoke to said, "We're here one week. Our two favorite places for entertainment are closed. We didn't come here to watch TV at night." Another person commented, "They're cleaning up one element and losing the rest."[50]

Not until 1966, after many impassioned hearings, did Weathering Heights get both its alcohol and entertainment licenses back. In June 1966, the club opened to a standing-room-only crowd.

The Columnist as Caped Crusader

It is not often that a newspaper columnist can play the hero.

In what for most people would be a fantasy from *The Secret Life of Walter Mitty*, Francis J. "Bossy" McGady, who wrote a column in the *Advocate* called "Up Along and Down Along," piloted a plane on July 19, 1950.[51] During a dinnertime flight between Provincetown and Boston, pilot Herbert E. Morse Jr., just twenty-one, realized that the landing gear was jammed. No problem. McGady took over the controls of the four-passenger Twin Cessna and circled in the skies for ninety minutes while Morse worked to free the landing gear. Down below, fire apparatus and ambulances assembled, as did reporters and photographers from all the Boston newspapers. Provincetown Airport manager John C. Van Arsdale flew to Boston in a BT-13 to join with others who were offering suggestions to the pilot from the tower. As time wore on and the Cessna began its second hour of circling, the scene resembled one from *It's a Mad, Mad, Mad, Mad World* in which Buddy Hackett and Mickey Rooney, at the controls of a small airplane, are "talked in" to a landing by an all-star cast in the control tower. As it turned out, McGady had some experience piloting small airplanes—back during the First World War in 1917. Morse finally resumed the controls and brought the plane in at an angle so that it favored the left wheel, which had descended. The landing at Logan Airport was rough, but no more so than others, the two passengers later said.

The *Provincetown Advocate* had been Provincetown's newspaper of record since 1869, and it was published on Thursday afternoons. The tone of a local newspaper should reflect the town it covers. It should be a paper of record when it comes to local politics, crimes and events, and it should, when appropriate, take a stance. It should mention as many names as possible in every story. Sometimes folksy, sometimes cantankerous, McGady's columns never failed to interest with their good-natured gossip and news—even at this distance of more than half a century. Although he owned and managed the Hotel Vernon of Worcester, he frequently visited Provincetown.

After his heroic time piloting the plane, McGady spent several weeks in a VA hospital in Framingham, apparently being treated for an ulcer or some other serious digestive ailment. To simplify his life, he soon left the hotel business to a relative and moved to Provincetown full time. All in all, McGady's two years or so of columns offer a wonderful picture of the tenor of Provincetown at that time.

On July 5, 1951, in welcoming McGady as a columnist, the *Advocate* described him as "a genial, white-thatched giant of a man" who traveled

The office of the *Provincetown Advocate* was behind the Advocate Postcard shop at 265 Commercial Street. The location, across from town hall, was convenient for a newspaper covering local politics. *Photo by the author.*

along Commercial Street "slowly, like a laden cargo ship." The thumbnail photo of McGady showed a man in a captain's hat with a cigar in his mouth. He would later be mistaken for the actor Sydney Greenstreet, who weighed nearly three hundred pounds. In his adopted town, McGady was known as a "genial host, chef par excellence, and raconteur." Who could ask for more in a columnist?

At the Flagship Restaurant, McGady spotted everyone from Montgomery Clift to the Marquis of Milford-Haven. He described swells from the New York Yacht Club in their navy blue jackets and baggy white linen shorts. "All the ladies came dripping with martinis and accents," McGady wrote in his column of August 16, 1951. And New York City psychiatrists beamed "like cats in the belfry of the Mission Capistrano upon the return of the swallows."

McGady wasn't afraid to offer his opinions on art here in this town where Hans Hofmann's school of abstract art held sway.

"We feel our desire to ridicule is greater than our desire to understand, and we do not wish to be unfair," McGady wrote on August 30, 1951. "We realize also that this town's greatest asset is a toss-up between the fishing business and the art colony."

A month later, celebrating his fifty-seventh—and final—birthday on September 25, McGady joined the Beachcombers for steaks at their clubhouse, "The Hulk." The Beachcombers Club is a group of male artists and hangers-on founded in 1916 to "promote good fellowship among men sojourning or residing in or about Provincetown who are engaged in the practices of fine arts or their branches." The group traditionally met each Saturday for dinner, trading off cooking duties. Following steaks with the Beachcombers, McGady moved on to the Flagship (The Hulk is attached to the Flagship) for "a roast, which was a symphony in beef." A cake was toted in. After all that eating, and no doubt drinking, it was perhaps fortunate that McGady lived in a first-floor apartment on Commercial Street across from the Flagship.

As another writer wrote in the *Advocate* a couple of days later, "We don't know what shape the beloved blimp is in today."

The "beloved blimp" weighed in himself, confessing that "the night ended with our ulcer hanging onto the lower intestines and glowing like a Vermont Central railroad depot stove in February."

By late December, McGady had recuperated from his birthday celebrations sufficiently to head out to the one cocktail party in town that's "a must," as he put it. This glittery affair was held in the home of Dr. and Mrs. Carl Murchison, Castle on the Hill. The Murchisons had hired a police officer to guard the gate against party crashers. McGady, who arrived in a taxi, came under special scrutiny "as to our resemblance to the ghost of Hermann Goring." Another guest, when stopped, asked if she had mistakenly arrived at the border of Budapest. World War II had ended, after all, just five years earlier.

Inside, McGady passed the evening by the punchbowl, eating the "prettiest hors d'oeuvres we have ever become tangled up with." The doctor's daughter, Marjorie, wore an elegant Hattie Carnegie designer gown that was the same color as the wine she was sipping (red). At midnight, McGady claimed he tossed an empty magnum of Peiper-Heidseck at the artist Philip Malicoat's head, "missing him by a yard and a half."

Sadly, McGady died the following March. "It is doubtful that there is anyone who knew him who did not have for him a deep and warm affection," the *Advocate* wrote.

Or, in the words of his friend the poet Harry Kemp, who wrote a poem called "In Memoriam," "He looked on living with a kindly sense / And held it wrong to stint its opulence."

Zoning and a Highway Come to Provincetown

From our perspective over sixty years down the road, it is hard to believe that most towns in postwar Massachusetts had neither planning boards nor zoning alliances. Zoning proposals met with fierce resistance in many towns, as residents asserted they had God-given rights to do as they wished with the land they had bought and now paid taxes on. Provincetown was no exception.

By the end of the war, in August 1946, the *Advocate* had come to see the merits of a planning board. Before the vote at town meeting in February 1947, the *Advocate* said planning boards are "what compass and helmsman are to a ship." While voters approved the board, legal challenges held it up for a couple of years until February 1949, when five members were elected to the board. This was a particularly crucial time for the town to have a voice in its own planning, as Route 6 was soon to enter Provincetown—but by what path?

In July 1949, the Massachusetts Highway Commission approved $8 million for a four-lane, limited-access highway that would run down the

Zoning laws protect these houses that "show influences of Greek Revival architecture on the independent thinking of the fishermen who designed them," Doris Doane wrote in *A Book of Cape Cod Houses. Painting by Deane Folsom Sr.*

spine of the Cape from the Sagamore Bridge to Provincetown. The work on the Mid-Cape Highway was scheduled to begin that very month.[52]

"The new highway can make or break Provincetown," the *Advocate* declared on July 7.

In September, with the planning board finally in place and plans moving along for Route 6, the topic of zoning again raised its head. In Massachusetts, 133 of 351 communities had zoning, including 3 on the Cape: Barnstable, Falmouth and Yarmouth. Zoning "can be made to work wonders with areas yet to be developed and which will become of great import when the new highway is extended around the town," the *Advocate* declared.

Voters at the February 1950 town meeting approved three zoning districts: residential, business and industrial. Once the zoning board was in place, a zoning board of appeals had to be established to deal with variances.

Evil Under the Sun

Just as the poet Harry Kemp had published his roman à clef, *Love Among the Cape Enders*, a generation earlier, now another novel with a Provincetown setting, *Evil Under the Sun*, again set tongues clucking. *Evil Under the Sun*, which appeared in August 1951, was called "a bitter indictment against almost everybody."

Evil Under the Sun—not to be confused with the 1941 Agatha Christie mystery of that title—was written by Anton Myrer, a Harvard graduate born in 1922. Myrer's wife, Judith Rothschild, was a student of Hans Hofmann.[53] In the late 1940s, Myrer was also a Provincetown summer resident and friend of Weldon Kees. Kees and his wife, Ann, had, in fact, proofed the book during the summer of 1950. As the tale unfolds, we meet a kaleidoscope of art students, teachers, sometimes-violent Portuguese fishermen and rich gay men.

Yet this is not the way Provincetown would care to show itself to the world. "Bossy" McGady weighed in early, calling the book the "personification of a 'stinkeroo.' If it was intended to depict Provincetown, then we must have been living under a wharf around here for the past 20 years or more," he wrote in the *Advocate* on September 27, 1951.

The sidewalks of the small town, where everyone lives cheek-by-jowl, are clogged with rich, teasing tourists. In between their art classes, the artists lie on the beach arguing about art and Freud.

While the main problem for Provincetown's 1950s boosters was that the book portrayed a sordid, dangerous town with a rotten underbelly, the main

One of the main characters in *Evil Under the Sun* moves into a small studio on a wharf modeled, no doubt, on Captain Jack's Wharf. *Painting by Oris Folsom.*

problem for the reader is that the book, 373 pages of dense prose often lapsing into a stream of consciousness, is peopled with unlikeable characters who all, rightly, detest one another. (As Mrs. Seever, the landlady repellently sums it up, after mulling over the town's year-round "Portagees" and summertime Jews, "If it isn't spiders it's ants.")

Perhaps something about Provincetown and its bohemian art colony just did not lend itself to high-quality fiction. Still, the novel remained required reading locally, with the Provincetown Bookshop dubbing it "a key-hole view of Provincetown Studio Life."

"Straight Gin, Please, and Just Spray the Room with Vermouth"

Despite—or because of—grim issues such as homophobia, polio, the Cold War and communism, the 1950s was the decade of the cocktail.

The cocktails of the day were Manhattans and martinis. "Bossy" McGady wrote a column on the Beachcombers' Thanksgiving party at The Hulk, noting that those were the prevalent cocktails and that they were "delicious." And the "Yak-ka-de Yak! sounded like the utter confusion at the Tower of Babel, nobody knew what the hell anyone else was talking about, and nobody cared, which is the way it should be," McGady wrote on November 22, 1951.

Harry Kemp tried to read a poem to mark the occasion, but as Kemp had forgotten his glasses and held the paper upside down, it was nonsense.

One of the "smartest" cocktail lounges opened at the end of June 1952—the new Thistle Room at the Bonnie Doone completed by Mr. and Mrs. Manuel Cabral. The theme of this lounge at 34 Bradford Street was "A Wee Bit of Scotland in Old Provincetown." The drink featured at the open house—and for many events that followed—was Harry Lauder Punch. And how do you make a Harry Lauder Punch? You mix Scotch whiskey (naturally), sweet vermouth and sugar syrup. Combine with ice. Shake well and strain into a cocktail glass.

"They are bringing an expert mixer here for the season from Casa Blanca, Florida, to build the king size cocktails to be served in the Thistle Room," the *Advocate* gushed on June 26, 1952.

Harry Lauder, by the way, was a Scottish entertainer known for "Roamin' in the Gloamin'."

Alcoholic punches were favorites throughout the decade, and sometimes the punch was Fish House Punch (served at the Flagship), Oriental Punch (at the Ho Hum) and, before the junior prom, fruit punch, presumably nonalcoholic.

In his 1954 *Peter Hunt's Cookbook*, Hunt offers the Flagship's recipe for Fish House Punch. It is a very simple concoction: "Dilute every 2 quarts of water with 1 quart Jamaica Rum, 1 quart Bacardi, 1 quart Cognac, ¾ pound sugar, 1 quart lemon juice." Simple but effective.[54] "They were plenty potent," someone told the *Advocate* after a party in 1940.[55]

What sort of hors d'oeuvres accompanied these mixed drinks? Sometimes they were plebian. "Before dinner Gardner prepared hors d'oeuvres, usually sliced salami and cheese on Triscuits, and drinks would be served," Reuel Wilson wrote of his father's friends and neighbors Ruth and Gardner Jencks.[56]

By the time television entered the lives of Provincetown's residents, it was a draw at the Bonnie Doone. "We are featuring Television and Hors d'oeuvres for the enjoyment and pleasure of our patrons," read an ad in the *Advocate* on August 26, 1954. By the way, "Lenny," the expert mixer, was still pouring those king-sized cocktails.

Hors d'oeuvre styles hummed along through the decade. For Jean Chrysler's birthday at the Atlantic House in September 1957, they were "fanciful," as well as "Portuguese," and served from early American wooden bowls. The food included spiced favas, stuffed sea clams with *linguica*, squid soup, *vina d'ahlos* tuna fish caught just the previous day in the harbor and Portuguese sweet breads and pastries.

"It took five native chefs two days to cook and prepare the delicacies that were served," the *Advocate* noted. One female guest was taken enough with the party to do a spontaneous flamenco dance with castanets.

At the Provincetown Arts Festival in July 1958, again the Portuguese hors d'oeuvres resurfaced. When the Ho Hum restaurant opened at 334 Commercial Street in June 1962, it served "Oriental punch and Chinese hors d'oeuvres."

At a party in July 1965, the hors d'oeuvres, served on "huge trays," were "fit to make a cigar store Indian drool."

And who could top that?

The Morning After

In his cookbook, Peter Hunt offers an antidote for the morning after. Here is his Prairie Oyster recipe:

> *With a small glass in your shaking hand, pour into it about a teaspoon of good vinegar and knock a shell-less egg into it. Add a sprinkle of Worcestershire sauce, and salt and pepper over all.*
> *Upsidaisy.*
> *If one's good, two's better.*[57]

Who Shall Run This Town?

Sometimes it seemed that everything was changing. For decades, Provincetown's municipal business had been run by a part-time, three-man board of selectmen on staggered three-year terms. Yet in 1951, after looking at other towns, the town appointed a town manager committee to study the administration of the town. Was the town being run as well as it could be? Could the tax rate be lowered with better management?

In 1953, voters at the annual Provincetown town meeting agreed to change the town's administration to a selectman-manager form of government. *Photo by the author.*

Would a manager bring greater efficiency and better long-range planning to the table?

After several months of study and debate, the committee decided that the current government was "completely out-dated." The committee recommended a manager, and the question went to voters at the annual town meeting on March 17, 1953. "Shall an act passed by the General Court in the year 1953 entitled 'An act to establish the Selectman-Manager form of government in the Town of Provincetown' be accepted by this Town?" After more than 1,000 voters cast ballots from noon to 6:00 p.m. in town hall, the answer was "yes" in favor of a town manager—541 to 469.

The Summer of '55: The Sun Gallery and New Energy

In 1955, Mary Heaton Vorse returned to Provincetown. Now eighty-one, "she did not deceive herself. She knew this homecoming was the final one."[58]

That summer, Mary McCarthy and her current husband, Bowden Broadwater, sometimes drove the fourteen miles from Wellfleet, where they had bought a house, to enjoy an after-dinner drink in Provincetown at the Atlantic House. Accompanying them was McCarthy's son Reuel Wilson—Reuel's father was Edmund Wilson—who, although only fifteen years old, had no trouble getting into the bars. Despite the ongoing battle with those who would "clean up" the town, the "Provincetown nightlife, with its all-female bands and transsexual performers, was quite an eye-opener," Wilson recalled.[59]

Meanwhile, a group of struggling young artists arrived to open the Sun Gallery at 393 Commercial Street to exhibit their work and stage "happenings." The Sun Gallery was one of several innovative galleries that opened in Provincetown at that time, and it brought with it a new energy. Shows hung for a week, from Monday evening to Sunday. Artists connected with the gallery included Dominic Falcone (who directed the Sun Gallery with his wife, Yvonne Andersen, until 1959), Jan Muller, Michael Hallett, Robert Gesner, Selina Trieff, John Frank, Larry Rivers, Alex Katz, Tony Vevers, Lester Johnson, Robert Beauchamp and the multimedia artist Red Grooms.

Born in Nashville, Tennessee, as Charles Rogers Grooms, Grooms came to Provincetown in the summer of 1957 to study with Hofmann. (His 1990 piece *Hofmeister* is a likeness of Hofmann.) He supported himself washing dishes at the Moors, and there he met Falcone, who dubbed him "Red" after his hair, and through him Andersen, with whom he began collaborating on experimental films.

Grooms's first solo show at the gallery was in August 1958. He incorporated in the show a session of himself painting for forty-five minutes—that was later dubbed "a happening."

One day, Falcone and twenty-one-year-old Grooms went to the library and got the librarian crowing. Grooms "is so young and so full of both art and energy that he left us with a new sort of zeal for both modern painting and modern living," Marion B. Haymaker wrote in her *Advocate* column "Books at the Library" on January 22, 1959.

The Landmark Fire of 1956

You could see the flames for many miles and out at sea when the Murchison house burned to the ground.

Carl Murchison had been a psychology professor at Clark University in Worcester. Born in 1887, he earned his PhD at Johns Hopkins University in 1923. In July 1936, after he resigned from Clark, he and his wife, Dorotea, bought the house in Provincetown where he continued to work in the field of psychology, publishing five journals. That same year, he began collecting art.

The Murchisons were traveling in Ecuador and had just reached Quito on the morning of May 2, 1956, when distressing news reached them. Their home, "The Castle," at the far West End, had burned down in an early morning fire the previous day. This was, of course, the house where columnist "Bossy" McGady had attended a very swish New Year's Eve party in 1951. As bad as the loss of the house was, the loss of Murchison's art collection, which included many early Provincetown painters, as well as old masters such as Reubens, Tintoretto and Gainsborough, was much worse. Murchison was an eclectic collector and also lost Venetian and Florentine glass, oriental rugs, "priceless antiques" and his psychology library.

The fire was estimated to have been burning for three to five hours before it was discovered by neighbor Wallace O'Donnell, who was getting ready to go fishing just before 4:30 a.m. The first alarm went out at 4:30 a.m. and the second ten minutes later. When firefighters arrived, the flames were breaking through the roof. The gates of a high iron fence that surrounded the estate were chained. A fire truck had to smash through the gates, losing more time.

The Red Inn was across the street from the Murchison house, "The Castle," which burned down in 1956. A modernistic house now sits on the hill above the harbor where the Pilgrims landed. *Collection of the author.*

"Two particularly violent heat blasts blew out all of the many windows, hurling glass as far as Commercial Street below and injuring several firemen slightly," the *Advocate* reported on May 3, 1956. "One blast lifted the high tower in the central building and dropped it into the flames." The explosions were compared to "ammunition such as shotgun shells and cartridges." It was speculated that faulty wiring caused the fire, which began in the basement.

It took an hour before fire chief Manuel White declared the fire under control—and then only after twelve streams of water were poured onto the house.

Upon receiving the unhappy news, the Murchisons immediately began their trek back to Provincetown and arrived home by the end of the week. At that point, the public developed an in-depth understanding of just what was lost in the fire. Lost were old masters that Dorotea inherited from her stepmother. Lost were 225 paintings, drawings and carvings and a "complete psychology textbook and research library." The loss was estimated at $250,000 in 1956 dollars.

By May 10, the couple had announced they planned to build "a completely modernistic home." For this they hired the Architects' Collaborative in Cambridge, a firm with which Walter Gropius was associated. The resulting modern house is often referred to as the "Gropius House," although it is likely that the firm's less famous architect Robert S. McMillan designed it.

A Chrysler Heir Gets Carded in a Garage

In July 1956, the "Personals" column in the *Advocate* mentioned a new face in town. It seemed that a "congenial customer" approached Chris Salvador, the boss at Marcy's Garage, and told him he wanted to open a charge account at the garage. Naturally, Salvador asked the stranger for an ID card. The name on the card? Walter P. Chrysler Jr.

Chrysler was born in Oelwein, Iowa, on May 27, 1909, and grew up on the North Shore of Long Island. His father, Walter P. Chrysler Sr., had founded the Chrysler Company in 1925. At the age of fourteen, the story goes, while a student at the Hotchkiss School, the younger Chrysler bought a small watercolor of a nude for $350.[60] That story was told not to illustrate that Chrysler had money to throw around but rather to illustrate his discerning eye for art. His dorm master destroyed the painting because he felt the nudity was inappropriate. Of course, the painting just happened to be by Renoir. Through the following years, Chrysler continued to collect art.

During the summer of 1956, Chrysler and his wife, the former Jean Esther Outland, whom he had wed in 1945, spent six weeks at Windcliffe at the Highlands in North Truro, a house belonging to Captain Wayne Duffet. Shortly before returning to New York in early August, the Chryslers hosted a clambake on the beach just below the house. Already, the Chryslers seemed to be fitting into Provincetown, as the *Advocate* noted that when a sudden thunderstorm hit, Mrs. Chrysler, who happened to be browsing in the library, helped lower the library's windows against the rain.

The following summer, the Chryslers were again back in town, and nine paintings from Chrysler's collection were on view at the Atlantic House from 4:00 to 6:00 p.m. every day except Saturdays. At the end of August, Chrysler hosted a surprise party for his wife in the Atlantic House taproom. Decorators worked from 9:00 a.m. to 4:00 p.m. filling the room with flowers and Japanese lanterns and weaving white and green streamers in and around the "fascinating collection of fishing relics that hang from the ceiling."[61] A three-tier birthday cake topped with a bayberry candle completed the decorations.

The A-list party included artists Henry Hensche, Hans Hofmann and Karl Knaths, all of whom arrived with their wives.

The home of the Chrysler Art Museum from 1958 to 1971, the Provincetown Public Library now occupies the 1861 church. A three-year renovation of the library was completed in 2005. *Photo by the author.*

The following month, Chrysler was touted as an "internationally known patron of the arts" who had the "largest private art collection in the world." His interest in Provincetown had been a "great stimulus to the colony." Perhaps, it was hoped, he might return the "art world spotlight" to Provincetown.

For a while, it looked as though just that would happen. On March 27, 1958, the parishioners of the Center Methodist Church voted to sell their church. The following month, it was transferred to Chrysler for $40,000. Chrysler "has talked about recapturing the glory that once belonged to Provincetown, where at the turn of the century it was reputed to be the art center of the universe."

Renovations to the interior of the building began. In early July, the Chryslers hosted a formal dinner for eighty-six. As guests sipped pre-prandial cocktails, they wandered through the museum admiring the displayed art. It was said that Chrysler often purchased the art of Provincetown painters in bulk.

It was perhaps ironic that an exhibit of 187 of Chrysler's paintings dated between 1850 and 1950 and called "The Controversial Century" went to Ottawa and caused a "situation of international dimensions" in October 1962. In his foreword to the exhibit's catalogue, Charles F. Comfort, the director of the National Gallery of Canada, wrote, "We look forward with great pleasure to its arrival in Canada. It is my opinion that it will contribute much to international understanding and amity."[62] Comfort's words were obviously written before the paintings arrived. It seemed that when the works were uncrated, various staff members at the National Gallery expressed doubt about "dubious attributions and poor painting." They questioned the authenticity of a Cezanne, a Degas, a Van Gogh, a Matisse, a Picasso and more—much more. The episode was an embarrassment of epic proportions.

By November 1962, *Life* magazine was calling the artworks "fakes" and "phonies." Because owning a fake and calling it genuine had tax implications, the investigation widened. And then Ralph F. Colin, administrative vice-president of the Art Dealers Association of America, came to Provincetown to examine the paintings after they were returned. While Chrysler might have been an "embarrassed and innocent victim of human error," Colin added that "no collector of Walter Chrysler's long experience could possibly be caught unawares with so many fakes from such unreliable sources."

The issue of whether the paintings were fakes was never fully resolved, but eventually, when the Chrysler Museum outgrew its space in Provincetown in 1971 and moved to a new location in Norfolk, Virginia, the questionable paintings were removed from display.

Only one person is known to have shimmied up the outside of the 253-foot Pilgrim Monument. *Painting by Katherine Baltivik.*

"The Human Fly" Scales the Pilgrim Monument

Imagine this: during a foggy July night in the summer of 1959, a twenty-year-old man shimmied up the outside of the Pilgrim Monument. Jonathan J. Thomas was, at the time of his death in 1978, the only person known to have scaled the 253-foot monument. Thomas used just his hands and feet—no mountain-climbing equipment—and it appeared that his sudden climb was a lark, a prank, just something to do as the fog swirled around the monument.

When he reached the top of the east wall, Thomas encountered a difficulty he had not foreseen in his concentration on his footholds and toeholds: he could not enter the monument because of bars welded over its windows. Now, at 2:15 a.m., he had to shout for help, and a taxi driver heard the shouts. Eventually, the Provincetown police climbed to the top of the monument—inside, using the stairs and ramps—and sawed through the bars to pull Thomas in.

In court, he was fined twenty-eight dollars for trespassing.

The tragic irony is that nineteen years later, Thomas fell fifteen feet from a roof he was working on and was, as a result, paralyzed from the neck down. He died at his home in Stowe, Vermont.[63]

3
From Beatniks to Hippies, 1960-1969

Land's-end places have always drawn those uneasy with society's conventions.
—New York Times, August 28, 1994

"Norman Mailer, You're Under Arrest"

If anyone got the 1960s off to a swinging start in Provincetown, it was Norman Mailer, the bestselling author of *The Naked and the Dead*. Already familiar with the landscape of Provincetown from a decade of summers in rental houses, during the summer of 1960, Mailer again rented the late Charles Webster Hawthorne's house on Miller Hill Road. This was the time when Mailer fought "anyone who would take him on," according to one of his biographers, Mary V. Dearborn.[64] Habits that Mailer had begun during the summer of 1959 continued into the summer of 1960. Drinking. Fighting. Pot smoking. Possibly nude cookouts.

It was before the season had even begun, on the night of June 9, when Mailer, walking with his second wife, Adele, back to Miller Hill after the bars closed, called out to a passing police car, "Taxi! Taxi!" The Provincetown police took this as enough of a provocation to shuttle Mailer to the police station in the cruiser. Somewhere along the way, the cops clubbed Mailer on the head—or he hit his head on the car's bumper. In any event, the town's doctor, Daniel Hiebert, sewed Mailer's scalp together with thirteen stitches. Adele bailed her husband out with fifty dollars.

Mailer represented himself at the trial and was eventually let off with a warning to be more polite to the police. The entire spectacle made its way into the *New Yorker* courtesy of the writer Dwight MacDonald, who summered in Truro and covered the trial.[65] During the following November, back in New York City, Mailer would have another well-publicized encounter with the police when he stabbed Adele in the stomach.

That summer of 1960, Adele Mailer was dancing in a production called *The Pirates of Provincetown.* She also had one spoken line, which was a scream.[66] This brings us to a relic of another era, Danton Walker.

Dying from Too Much Cha-cha-cha

In July 1960, Danton Walker came to Provincetown for a two-week revival of his musical comedy originally called *Cod's Own Country*, which had been presented at Mary Bicknell's Wharf Theater in 1927. In 1960, the play, renamed *The Pirates of Provincetown*, was opening at Playhouse on the Wharf, and with its riffs on artists and theater people mingling with locals in the "Conge Vous" nightclub, the play was said to be "hilarious."

Walker, who was born in 1889, comes straight out of the fast-talking comedies of the '40s, like *The Man Who Came to Dinner*. In fact, the main character of that film, Sheridan Whiteside, was based on Walker's boss, the fat, acerbic theater critic Alexander Woollcott.

Walker, too, became a Broadway theater critic in the 1930s, one of those mythical figures all playwrights and actors fear because they can make or break a play according to their reviews the morning after opening night. Walker was a regular summer visitor to Provincetown, and as an observer of the town for nearly four decades, he often wrote about it in his syndicated column in the *New York Daily News*, much to the displeasure of Provincetown's newspaper-reading public.

"You can hardly smell the salt air for the gasoline fumes, and now they talk of gutting the center of the town to make room for more cars," he wrote in a 1954 column that enraged just about everyone.[67] He added that the beaches where art classes were once held were now parking lots.

At any rate, by the summer of 1960, when Walker put on his revival, he seemed to have reached a truce with townsfolk. And then he suffered a heart attack, while staying at the Sea Horse Inn, on August 3, the same day he had planned to attend the annual Beachcombers Ball.

By the time Danton Walker criticized the town as being clogged with cars, scenes of cod set out to dry just about everywhere were long gone. *Collection of the author.*

In his final newspaper column, he wrote that his heart attack was brought on by "too much cha-cha-cha."

When he died on August 11, his friend Helen Bishop wrote that "the third act curtain, for him, came down fast."[68]

His obituaries seemed to wink when they stated that Walker, who was dubbed "Dapper Dan" and best recalled wearing evening clothes, was a "bachelor."

The Death of the Last Bohemian

On the morning of August 8, 1960, Harry Kemp, seventy-six, died. After years of living alone in a rough dune shack, Kemp spent his last days in a small cottage on Howland Street "built for him practically single-handedly" by his friend Sunny Tasha. When public health nurse Grace Atkins stopped in at about 10:00 a.m. during her rounds, she found Kemp near death. Atkins summoned Dr. Daniel Hiebert and the Provincetown rescue. Kemp died at 11:00 a.m. The official cause of death was a cerebral hemorrhage, the *Advocate* reported on August 11.

The irony is that Kemp was a man who would have adored the decade of the 1960s. His biographer, William Brevda, dubbed Kemp the "last bohemian." "At midcentury, Kemp was a living relic of a vanished past," Brevda wrote. "He still cherished and fought for the bohemian values of youth, anarchistic self-expression, unabashed exuberance, and enthusiasm." Kemp "was the last of his group to acknowledge the wreck of his youthful dreams."[69]

Kemp was born in Youngstown, Ohio, in 1883. In one of the strangest interludes of the first third of his life, he was enmeshed in a lengthy love triangle/divorce scandal with novelist Upton Sinclair and Sinclair's wife, Meta, in 1911. Eventually, after months of newspaper headlines, Kemp dubbed the scandal "a great romance."

Kemp was nearly thirty-four when he first visited Provincetown with his wife, the actress Mary Pyne, during the summer of 1916. A decade later, Kemp began his roman a clef, *Love Among the Cape Enders*, loosely based on that summer.

Kemp's entire life spoke to a bohemian bent. In the summer of 1927 or 1928, he moved to a ten- by ten-foot shack in the dunes of Peaked Hill and stayed there every summer for the next thirty years. When Edmund Wilson was living in the Peaked Hill Life-Saving Station, Eugene O'Neill's former house down on the backside of the Cape, his daughter Rosalind, who was born in 1924, frequently saw Kemp. Many years later, she ran into him around town and remarked on his out-of-step quality.

"He became a travesty of himself, a Provincetown landmark with a great black cape, proclaiming himself 'the dune poet,'" she recalled in her memoir *Near the Magician*. "I never was quite sure who he was; he was simply there, a leftover from a childhood scene in which all the other grown-up characters had moved on."[70]

In December 1952, Kemp led a *Boston Globe* reporter, Willard DeLue, along an "Indian trail" out to the dune shack. DeLue remarked that you could easily become disoriented on a foggy day and that on a day of fierce wind, the blowing sand could draw blood. When the pair finally reached the shack, DeLue noted it was locked with only a simple padlock. A sign on the door advised: "There is nothing of value except solitude." Inside the shack, DeLue described a shelf of books, a table, a cot, an oil stove, a coffee pot and pans, a couple of chairs and a lamp. "Spare food in bags hung from the rafters," and it was cold.[71]

On November 21, 1947, Kemp first reenacted the Pilgrims' 1620 landing in Provincetown Harbor. His goal, according to Brevda, was "to debunk

On his birthday on December 15, the poet Harry Kemp always took a dip in frigid Provincetown Harbor. *Photo by Deane Folsom II.*

and dispel 'the hoax of the rock'"—that is, Plymouth Rock, which seemed always to garner more glory as the first place the Pilgrims set foot than the rightful spot, Provincetown. Another of Kemp's obsessions was the Pilgrim women's first Monday washday, and he gleefully reenacted that, too.

Kemp's birthday was December 15, and in 1953, according to his custom, he took a birthday dip in frigid Provincetown Harbor. In 1959, when his wintertime landlord, John Francis Jr., died, he was evicted from what was called Francis Flats, home to Eugene O'Neill and so many other writers and artists in their salad days. That was when Tasha built him his house.

Kemp made headlines after his death when Tasha attempted to carry out his final wish, which was to be cremated. After Tasha shipped his body to the crematory, a group of "prominent Provincetown citizens" demanded the body for a "proper Catholic burial." State police were dispatched to bring Kemp's body back to Provincetown. Eventually, Tasha prevailed when she produced "a legal document that named her executrix to Kemp's last will and estate."[72] Tasha and other friends scattered half of Kemp's ashes over Peaked Hill and the other half in Greenwich Village, mainly in front of the Provincetown Playhouse on MacDougal Street.

If, as Brevda says, "time has forgotten Harry Kemp," he is remembered in Provincetown in a street called Harry Kemp Way off Conwell Street.

"Artist-Broke"

In July 1962, a panel of six residents sat down to discuss the topic "Provincetown—Summer Art Capital of the USA." The previous year, the Provincetown Museum had been built by the Pilgrim Monument.

The article contended that in the summer, Provincetown's population swelled to five times its winter population of 3,500—or to 17,500 people. (Many more were to come during later summers.) This brought out the usual griping. "This is a small New England town, a religious fishing community, and we welcome you," said lawyer John C. Snow, a 1937 Provincetown High graduate. Yet some summer people "behave here as they wouldn't in their own communities."

Artist Karl Knaths recalled how in his early days in town a heap of garbage was always lying just outside his door. When he complained to his neighbor, who happened to be the police chief, the chief said, "I've always thrown it there, and I'm going to keep on throwing it there."

So what was it that lured Knaths to Provincetown?

"Like myself, the first painters came here because they were 'artist-broke,'" he said. For thirty dollars a year, he was able to rent a studio in "an old sail loft reeking of salt cod and cluttered with junk." Furthermore, compared to city life, "there were no 'verboten' signs."

The Provincetown Art Association and Museum (PAAM) was founded in 1914 and boasts an enormous permanent collection of Provincetown art. During the summer of 2014, PAAM celebrates its centennial. *Photo by Deane Folsom II.*

Interestingly, he considered Provincetown not an indigenous art colony but an "adjunct of the New Yorkopolis."

In contrast, Walter Chrysler, who with his wife founded the Chrysler Art Museum, called Provincetown the "most active art colony in the country." "The town had a kind of life we both very much like," he said, and a "perhaps" superior intellectual atmosphere. The town was also cosmopolitan.[73]

Playwright Abe Burrows, who won a Pulitzer Prize for Drama that year, for *How to Succeed in Business Without Really Trying*, added that in recent years most of his plays were written in Provincetown.

That same summer, Robert Motherwell was creating a series of sixty-four abstract oil paintings called "Beside the Sea" and mainly in blues, yellows, browns and greens. His violent method of splashing oil paint against rag paper (specially reinforced with five layers of glue) was intended to replicate the spray of seawater against a building. This sight was something with which Motherwell was intimately familiar, as the water hit the seawall outside his house/studio at 631 Commercial Street. During the summer of 1962, he and his third wife, artist Helen Frankenthaler, worked in a studio at Days Lumberyard, long the venue of the town's artists.

Motherwell had bought a cottage at 631 Commercial and transformed it into a three-story house/studio with a distinctive flat roof. The *Advocate*, on April 11, 1963, decried that and other changes in the East End. "The public seems to be threatened by a loss of the old Provincetown, cherished for its quaintness."

The Day JFK Was Shot

In Provincetown, it was Frances Raymond, chief operator at the Provincetown switchboard, who first felt the rippling effects of President John F. Kennedy's assassination in Dallas. At the switchboard, "suddenly every line flared red," and Raymond was compelled to call in all off-duty operators as Provincetown residents, reacting to JFK's death, called friends and relatives.

The streets were empty and quiet, as everyone stayed inside, glued to the radio and television. That evening, the Church of Saint Mary of the Harbor, among other churches, held a memorial service. Schools, most offices and shops were closed on Monday, the day of Kennedy's funeral. Churches again held services and masses.

"Even now Provincetown is quiet, drained of emotion, and still unbelieving," the *Advocate* reported on November 28.

Today, fifty years later, we wonder how history was altered by those fatal shots in Dallas. Can we ascribe to the assassination the profound societal changes that followed almost immediately? Was the assassination "the catalyst for an era of turmoil, discord, and bloodshed, Vietnam, campus unrest, the assassinations of Martin Luther King and Robert Kennedy, race riots, the rise of the counterculture and a surge in drug abuse, even the toxic political climate that gave rise to Watergate?"[74]

A couple of weeks after the assassination, a plan to rename a portion of the new Cape Cod National Seashore in memory of JFK drew sour letters to the editor of the *Advocate*. "For every vote for Mr. Kennedy there was one for Nixon," S. Osborn Ball, a Provincetown attorney wrote on December 5. Ball said the dust needed to settle on Kennedy's presidency as it had on Abraham Lincoln's before memorializing the late president. Ball provoked a flurry of letters emphasizing Kennedy's greatness.

By Christmas, flags were no longer flying at half-mast. Yet the Christmas spirit was "dampened," the *Advocate* noted the day after Christmas. For one thing, the Pilgrim Monument, always lighted from top to bottom with colored lights, was dark due to the state's order that the town could not spend money on private property. (The monument was owned by the Cape Cod Pilgrim Association.) The dark monument, which could no longer be glimpsed from windows or "from out to sea or returning along Route 6," seemed to symbolize an entire nation in mourning.

The National Seashore Comes to Town

During July 1964, nearly a half million visitors tramped through the Cape Cod National Seashore. This was the second summer of the seashore, and by now, the *New York Times* reported on August 30, 1964, Cape Codders' hostility to the park had abated.

Today, most people are so grateful for the open space preserved at the Cape Cod National Seashore that they forget that when it was first proposed, it was met with blazing controversy in the six towns it touched: Provincetown, Truro, Wellfleet, Eastham, Orleans and Chatham.

The story of a proposed National Seashore first broke in the *Cape Codder* newspaper on November 1, 1956.

In one of the earliest articles on the proposed seashore, the *Advocate* spoke in its favor. The public awaited the result of a yearlong study on the "taking" of thirty thousand acres along the Atlantic shoreline, including about seventy acres that encompassed the eight square miles of dunes in Provincetown and Truro. The National Park Service described the seventy acres as "a triangular area adjacent to Route 6 and straddling Race Point Road."[75] "The time is ripe to think of what it will mean to future generations if a substantial part of outer Cape Cod is set aside in this manner to be preserved for all time," the *Advocate* noted on January 16, 1958. "The benefits will accrue to all of us, from Truro to Texas."

In April 1959, a petition opposing the National Seashore was placed in Dorothy's Gift Shop in Provincetown. The thrust of this petition was that, while the "undersigned" favored a National Park, they "strongly opposed…the taking of our year round homes, summer homes and places of business." The petitioners called for a smaller-scale park.

One of the arguments against the park revolved around the "transient sightseer who comes over on the Boston boat or drives down the Cape to buy cheap souvenirs and rubberneck from his car."[76] On other parts of the Cape,

Hot dog lovers came to exemplify the type of tourists some snobs said they did not want to draw to town. This eatery is near MacMillan Wharf. *Photo by the author.*

where the "transients" did not vomit forth from a daily boat, the "hotdog stand" crowd was invoked as the ultimate in lowlifes. The fear was that a national park might attract even more of the rubbernecking hot dog lovers. One Truro resident dubbed the proposed seashore a "rape of the Cape." He noted, in fact, that the "honky-tonks and the like" are all outside the boundaries of the proposed seashore and that the attractive homes, "like our Blueberry Hill," are inside the seashore.[77]

In July 1959, Jean Outland Chrysler, wife of Walter P. Chrysler Jr., writing as a "the wife of a property owner in Wellfleet and Provincetown," sent a lengthy letter opposing the park to President Dwight D. Eisenhower and other politicians, including U.S. representative John F. Kennedy. Chrysler called the creation of the park "tyrannical destruction of the right of citizens to own, improve, dispose of, bequeath or will property," referring to what she

The National Park Service offers residencies for artists and writers in the rustic Dune Shacks of Peaked Hill Bars Historic District. *Painting by Deane Folsom Sr.*

assumed was the fate of property within the seashore. She took particular issue with a *New York Times Magazine* article published on May 3 that used the term "The Vanishing Shoreline." Again, more than a whiff of elitism entered the argument against a national seashore:

> *The term "vanishing shoreline" is a very accurate phrase to describe what is to happen to thirty thousand and more acres of land made accessible to an estimated forty million people who can plan to invade the Cape with nothing more in their pockets than enough to pay for gasoline to return home, leaving their trash and refuse as a grim reminder of their visit.*

Chrysler wound up her letter by saying that the "seizure" of the land was undemocratic and added that it was a "shocking example" for those who had been persecuted outside the United States.

By September 24, 1959, the *Advocate* had pretty much gelled its arguments against the National Seashore by saying the best way to "save the Cape from hoods, hot-rodders, litter-bugs and fire-bugs" was to keep these lands in private hands. "Once the tract is in the hands of the Federal government the Lower Cape will be in the hands of political absentee landlords who can and who will handle the area as they see fit."

On March 13, 1961, voters at Provincetown's annual town meeting voted on Article 53. Article 53 consisted of four questions designed to "see if the Town will express its opinion on the following questions relative to the establishment of the Cape Cod National Seashore Park."[78] Townspeople voted two to one in favor of the park.

Finally, on August 7, 1961, President Kennedy signed the bill creating the 43,607-acre Cape Cod National Seashore.

The UFO Over Pilgrim Lake

Through the years, many unexplained phenomena have been observed at the Cape's tip. Take the case of abstract expressionist Budd Hopkins, an influential figure in the New York art world, as well as among the coterie of intellectuals summering in Provincetown, Truro and Wellfleet. One summer evening in August 1964, he; his wife, Joan; and a houseguest were driving to Provincetown to a party. Imagine the big American car with its giant steering wheel and the two men in the front seat, with Joan Hopkins between them, as it barreled along the hard asphalt of Route 6. It was 5:15 p.m., and the sky was clear. The trio was just passing Pilgrim Lake when a "small, lens-shaped object [appeared] in the sky ahead of us," Hopkins wrote. Hopkins braked as the three of them observed the object as it hovered in the sky over the dunes, moving in front of and behind clouds before it took off "at the speed of a small airplane" into a cloudbank over the ocean. When they arrived at the party, Hopkins mentioned the mysterious aircraft to some of the other guests, among whom were the poet Mary Oliver and her partner, Molly Malone Cook. Oliver and Cook said that they, too, had seen such a metallic object over Route 6.

Hopkins came to believe that it was "some kind of probe from 'elsewhere,' a piece of advanced observational equipment." About a decade later, Hopkins began interviewing people he believed had been abducted by aliens.

In the 1980s, a group met at Herring Cove to scan the night skies for UFOs and, over time, saw plenty. In October 1974, two young men claimed to have "lost time" in the wee hours of the morning at Herring Cove and to have found inexplicable bruises the size of pencil erasers on their chests.[79]

Provincetown's Dr. Feelgood

Who knows the dark secrets and hidden tangles of a town better than its doctor?

Dr. Daniel H. Hiebert came to Provincetown in 1919 as a newly minted, newly wed general practitioner, and through five decades, until his death at the age of eighty-three in 1972, Hiebert treated the town's residents, sailors and famous visitors alike.

A native of Hillsboro, Kansas, Hiebert came east to study at Boston University Medical School. In a bizarre coincidence, Hiebert and Eugene O'Neill both boarded with the Ebel family. (Hiebert's sister had married one of the Ebels.)[80]

Not long after that, in 1919, Hiebert set up practice from his house at 322 Commercial Street. O'Neill's wife, Agnes Boulton, described Hiebert, who delivered her baby Shane, as "big and young and kindly."

At one time or another, just about everyone in town was treated in Dr. Daniel Hiebert's office, located in his home at 322 Commercial Street. *Photo by the author.*

In later years, Hiebert was often called upon to reminisce about "his efforts to keep O'Neill sober long enough to write his first full-length production *Beyond the Horizon*."[81]

Despite what must have been the heavy burden of his perpetually on-call medical practice, Hiebert managed to have his finger in many pots in town. He was an American Legion commander. He was a U.S. Public Health officer, responsible at times for determining the health of those stepping off the many ships in the harbor. He bought Captain Jack's Wharf in 1936 and began upgrading it. He was, for over twenty years, the county medical examiner. And he was down at the West End of Commercial Street on November 21 every year with Harry Kemp, reenacting the Pilgrims' landing.

"It was all somewhat silly, but it did keep the true history alive," Hiebert's only child, Ruth, said many years later about the reenactment.[82]

Hiebert was said to neither drink nor smoke. He rose at six thirty every morning and saw between twenty and thirty patients a day. He landed by helicopter on the deck of a fishing vessel and worked a nineteen-hour stint putting together the survivors of a Nazi submarine attack during World War II. In 1960, he was named General Practitioner of the Year by the Commonwealth of Massachusetts.

Julia Whorf Kelly remembered that when she broke her nose on a metallic swing set in the 1950s, she was brought immediately to Hiebert's office. She recalled with particular clarity that "the wallpaper was a detailed street scene of an English fishing port drawn in maroon-colored lines on a cream colored background."

The doctor's wife was his assistant, and he always called her "Mother." Hiebert set Kelly's nose and then rebroke it a week later because it was "crooked." A week after that, he removed the stitches. She has only a tiny scar to this day.[83]

That was all before the swinging, psychedelic 1960s, when things got really weird.

Film director John Waters, in a 2011 interview, dubbed Hiebert "Dr. Feelgood."

"The pills came from Dr. Hiebert...the notorious Dr. Feelgood of Provincetown. He seemed to have given diet pills to everyone in the town. I think he didn't know that everyone was getting high. But I was six-foot-one and weighed 130 pounds. It was kind of hard to think I should go on a diet."[84]

Waters sold the pills on the street, from his bike. That was in 1967 or 1968.

Waters's friend the actress Mary Vivian Pearce related the same story. "I told him I wanted to be a model, for an acting part," she recalled. "He said, 'Okay, do you want the strong pills?'" The "strong pills" were speed, or "black beauties." "He was very old, and fell asleep examining people," Pearce added.

By 1969, Hiebert's waiting room was very plain and stocked with well-thumbed *National Geographics*. His big oak desk was cluttered with medical magazines, unopened mail, an ancient microscope and a bag of lollipops. He was said to have delivered 1,400 babies—but who was counting by then?[85]

In June 1966, a medical center opened in Wellfleet on Route 6 and attracted two "permanent" physicians, offering at least a little competition to Hiebert.[86]

When Hiebert died in 1972, after a fifty-three-year stint as the town's doctor, one columnist wrote, "It's common knowledge that half of the population of Provincetown was delivered by Dr. Hiebert." "Doctor Hiebert was a one-man band," Francis Santos told the *Cape Cod Times* in 2005. He delivered four of Santos's six children, right there in Santos's house.[87] "There's never been a man like him. He'd come to your house any hour of the day or night. He was dedicated. More than a regular person."

At land's end, with Cape Cod Hospital about fifty miles away, there was no doubt that it was necessary to keep a doctor nearby.

"He used to make his own medicines," resident Robert Harrison recalled. "He would mix something up and charge you for it."

It was said that "sometimes he refrained from billing people; other times he tried to take patients' property when they were on their deathbeds."[88]

Harrison was more blunt.

"He would stop at the late lamented's house and collect his bill," he recalled. "'You know that piece of property in Truro?'" The doctor would also accept jewelry in lieu of cash. Harrison gleefully recalled one incident in which one of the diamonds Hiebert took as his postmortem fee turned out to be fake.

"How Much Flour Goes in Gravy?"

"When is high tide?"

"Can you connect me with Happy's mother?" "Pie Alley?" "Tootsie?" "Iron Man?" "Squid?" "Hommanaka?" "Manny the Hasp?" "Doombie?"

"How long does it take to cook a pork chop?"

"What day is it?"

These were all questions fielded by Provincetown's switchboard operators in the New England Telephone and Telegraph office at 100 Bradford Street. As of April 1966, when Provincetown became the last town on Cape Cod to move to an automated system, the questions would no longer be answered. In fact, "a whole deep pool of immortal dialogue between [residents] and the Provincetown switchboard operators will have dried up."[89]

In the classic 1966 movie *The Russians Are Coming, The Russians Are Coming,* set on a small island off Cape Cod, we see a telephone operator, Alice Foss, sitting alone at a switchboard arguing with the police chief, conveying information and gossip. The Russians finally gag Foss and tie her to summer resident Walt Whittaker for her troubles.

The sixteen operators at the local switchboard—a number that jumped to twenty-four in the summer—would be retired, or let go, when the office was automated. Anyone pressing "0" on his or her telephone would be referred to Hyannis, where the operator was unlikely to know who "Hommanaka" was, never mind "Hommanaka's" number.

The trouble was, so many residents shared the same name—there were at least a dozen Joseph Souzas in the 1950s—that nicknames were the sole way to differentiate them. And what creative names they were: "Joe Spaghetti," "Eddie Boozy," "Jazz Garter," "Big He," "Bottles Souza," "Scarry Jack," "Willie Alle," "Piggy-Wee," "Mary Goddam," "Slim Perry" and the easy-to-remember "Rat."[90]

Incredibly, local subscribers would not only have to come up with the formal name that might be printed in a telephone directory, but they'd also "be on their own as they learn the routine of dialing seven digits to complete their calls." For many of the elderly, who were used to their local operators calling their doctors or helping them "with some personal problem," the switchover was expected to be more complicated than for younger folk. "You'll dial 487 and you're on your own" to fill in the subsequent four digits.

Over a decade before the conversion, on August 30, 1951, columnist "Bossy" McGady offered the telephone operators a "verbal nosegay." He predicted that when the dial system was eventually put into use, "it will take at least a year for the townsfolk to become acclimated to these instruments."

After the conversion, one woman complained that she was awakened at 4:45 a.m. by a wrong number. One "poor old man" now sits staring at his telephone instead of being able to call for a taxi. "And that mechanical buzz"—the dial tone—"is such a cold, impersonal thing after many years of a friendly voice at the other end."[91]

If a man were out fishing, the switchboard operators at the Provincetown Telephone and Telegraph office would most likely inform the caller that he was unavailable. *Photo by Deane Folsom II.*

Frances Raymond retired as the head of the office, a position she had held for a decade. Raymond came from a family of six; her parents were from the Azores. In a 1958 interview, she was described as "a charming soft-spoken lady." That year, 7,300 calls were "pegged" each day. In the summer, the number ballooned to 12,500 a day. Through those years, well before the 911 emergency system was even dreamed of, the women were also credited with acting in a timely way to find firemen who were in church services, for example. They also worked through blizzards without light and heat, connecting families.

On that same day, April 17, when Vineyard Haven and Edgartown on Martha's Vineyard became automated, the "last links in what will be the completed New England dial system" were connected.[92]

A May-December Marriage and a Muse

Sometimes when a very old widower weds a woman about a third of his age, he finds a caregiver. Or maybe he's not used to living alone, after a marriage of sixty years that ended abruptly with the death of his wife.

In the case of Hans Hofmann, it seems he found a muse.

In April 1963, Maria Wolfegg Hofmann, "Miz," died of a heart attack after gallbladder surgery. A few months later, as the story goes, back in Provincetown, Hofmann's neighbors introduced Hofmann to a thirty-three-year-old woman from Germany named Renate Schmitz. Soon, Hofmann began his late great cycle of paintings, "The Renate Series." The paintings, which were all done in 1965, "may be seen as the final summation of the themes, thoughts, and stylistic inventions with which Hofmann was so successfully concerned in the last years of his life," Henry Geldzahler, curator of twentieth-century art at the Metropolitan Museum of Art, wrote in the catalogue for the series. He called Hofmann "an artist who had his genius, turbulent and shining as it was, under full control and under his command."[93]

Hofmann had closed his schools in Provincetown and New York to concentrate on his own painting in 1958, and in 1963, the Museum of Modern Art gave Hofmann a one-man retrospective show.

In talking about "The Renate Series," one thinks of Andrew Wyeth's "The Helga Pictures." Yes, Hofmann's works were abstract expressionist in style and not representational. And yes, Hofmann painted 9 works to Wyeth's 240. The differences continue, yet the muse's strong influence hovers over both projects.

Almost all of the titles of Hofmann's nine paintings can be interpreted as having erotic overtones: *Rhapsody, Lonely Journey, Little Cherry, Legends of Distant Past Days, Heraldic Call, Profound Longing, Deep Within the Ravine, Summer* and, finally, *Lust and Delight.*

Hofmann, then eighty-five, married Schmitz in October 1965 and continued with his cycle of works. On February 17, just four months later,

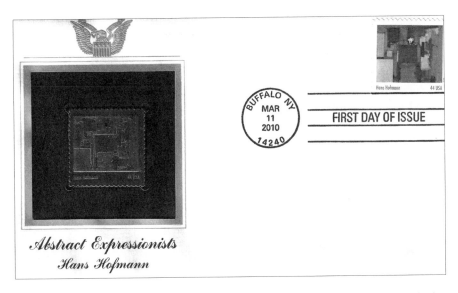

This 2010 Hans Hofmann stamp was part of the U.S. Postal Service's abstract expressionist series. The series also includes Robert Motherwell and Jackson Pollock. *Collection of the author.*

Hofmann died of a heart attack, and Schmitz, so recently a bride, became a widow, planning a funeral for a major artist in New York City.

In his obituary, the *New York Times* called Hofmann "the leading figure behind the emergence of abstract expressionism as the dominant style of American painting after the end of World War II."[94]

During the fall after Hofmann's death, thieves broke into the Hofmann home in Provincetown and stole forty-two artworks by Hofmann and other artists. The thieves were believed to be professionals, as they "exercised considerable discrimination in their choice of paintings, selecting the most valuable," the *Advocate* reported on December 15, 1966. Because the paintings were by such artists as Juan Miro, Jackson Pollock and Georges Braque, as well as Hofmann, it was assumed the thieves would realize they were too hot to sell except through the "international black market." Yet within just three months the forty-one paintings and one lithograph were found in a New Haven motel after one of the thieves negotiated with an FBI agent, thinking he was an insurance agent. Two Springfield, Massachusetts lawyers were arrested and charged with interstate transportation of stolen property. Later, two Provincetown men were charged with breaking and entering into the Hofmann home and the theft of the paintings.

And what of Hofmann's young widow? When a muse is no longer a muse, the muse can be devastated. Take the case of Helga Testorf, whom Andrew Wyeth painted secretly between 1972 and 1985. As Wyeth completed the cycle of paintings and drifted apart from Helga, she fell into a clinical depression. One day, Wyeth's wife, Betsy, met Helga in Wyeth's studio. "In the corner was a kind of bed and there's a lot of potato chips and boxes of Cheez Whiz and this figure is slowly pulling itself up…She doesn't say a word, just sort of stood, looking me up and down," Betsy Wyeth recalled.[95]

Renate Hofmann dropped out of the public eye for several decades, dying in 1992. In 2001, gruesome details of her life emerged when court papers revolving around a 1998 lawsuit against her guardians were unsealed. Because of "emotional disturbances," a New York county superior court had appointed "co-committees" of Renate Hofmann's assets, which were estimated at over $50 million. (Hans Hofmann's work continued to appreciate. After 2000, several of his paintings were auctioned by Sotheby's New York for nearly $800,000 each.)[96] Renate Hofmann's final days were hashed over in the *New York Daily News* under headlines such as "From Caviar to Cat Food." Hofmann was described as a "wealthy but paranoid schizophrenic widow living with her cats and liquor in a garbage-strewn oceanfront" Florida home, neglected by all, malnourished and lacking in medical care.[97] The suit was settled out of court.

Hans Hofmann and his two wives are buried in Snow Cemetery in Truro. In her will, Renate created the Renate, Hans and Maria Hofmann Trust to promote the study of Hofmann and his art.

Death of Pioneer Mary Heaton Vorse

A gull in flight and a seahorse are carved into the red granite of Mary Heaton Vorse's headstone in the Provincetown Cemetery.[98]

On June 14, 1966, Vorse rose early and read the newspapers in bed in the Commercial Street house she had lived in for fifty-nine years. At noon, her son Heaton brought her lunch in bed. He then went out to run errands, and when he returned, he found his mother still in bed, dead of a heart attack, with the newspapers spread out around her. She was ninety-two.

In her obituary, the *New York Times* described Vorse as a "newspaper woman, novelist, and militant liberal."[99] Just a few years earlier, she had helped organize a protest against the dumping of nuclear waste.[100] And in

Journalist Mary Heaton Vorse (1874–1966) is often credited with leading the literary crowd to Provincetown. She is buried in Provincetown Cemetery. *Photo by the author.*

1965, she backed the town's young Episcopal minister in his march against the Vietnam War.

Vorse's funeral at the Church of Saint Mary of the Harbor was small, as the funerals of the aged who have outlived their friends often are.

Surviving Vorse were Heaton; his half brother Joel O'Brien of Westport, Connecticut; their sister, Mary Ellen Boyden of New York City; and three grandchildren.

With the deaths of Susan Glaspell, Harry Kemp and Vorse, the generation of Eugene O'Neill, who died in 1953, and the Provincetown Players had ended.

Rebels Against Personal Hygiene

Provincetown's reputation as a welcoming place, a haven at land's end for the nonconformist, again began to agitate some of the local people as the summer of 1965 began. Sixty residents, headed by baker and restaurateur Napoleon Eugene Poyant, brought a petition to the selectmen, asking the board to make "unwelcome," apparently through the strict interpretation of existing laws, rules and regulations, a certain type of person who fell under the rubric "beatnik."[101] Considering that Greenwich Village was a mecca for beatniks—they are "found like mushrooms in Greenwich Village"— it was not surprising that beatniks should move to Provincetown, the village's summer residence.[102]

There was no doubt that the beatnik population was increasing. On February 20, 1964, a letter to the editor from Dr. Norman E. Zinberg of Boston asserted that while Zinberg and his wife had been coming to their home in Provincetown now for six years, there seemed to be a "great influx of tourists who are either of the beatnik type or stuffy and who do not contribute to the unique and special quality of Provincetown." The good doctor's solution to this problem? Prevent the construction of proposed four-story motels in the East End.

In August 1964, a Mr. and Mrs. Eliotrope of Ludlow had complained to the town manager that they had docked at MacMillan Wharf in their cabin cruiser for the night, only to be kept up until the early hours of the morning by a "noisy group of 'beatniks'" who were holding a party in a boat tied up near theirs.[103]

But what is a beatnik? Town manager Robert A. Hancock said he, for one, did not know. "There are people who let their hair grow and may be considered different from the common run, but [just] because they don't wear shoes, you can't have a special set of laws for them."

Police chief Francis H. Marshall apparently agreed with Hancock. "We have many characters who need a shave, bath and who run around with long hair, sometimes referred to as nonconformists. If they choose to rebel against society in personal hygiene, that's all right, as long as they do not become nonconformists to our laws," he said.

The eminent artist Ross Moffett now stepped up to the plate, complaining about a "motorcycle venture" that would only augment the terrible traffic snarls on Commercial and Bradford Streets. "It should be plain that there is just so much room in these narrow streets," wrote the author of the 1964 *Art in Narrow Streets*. He invoked an image of Hell's Angels, "roving bands of mounted beatniks," menacing Provincetown's streets.[104]

Still, although resident Lewis C. Richardson held "no brief for beatniks," he found upholding principles of democracy to be more important than ridding the town of "distasteful" persons.[105]

The word "hippie" was just a few months in the future.[106] The hippie movement was not far down the road, and the longhaired, shoeless style was about to become ever more prevalent.

In the summer of 1966, a Provincetown street artist, encountered one evening on Commercial Street, sketched the author on gold foil. He signed his work "Raso." *Collection of the author.*

The story took on a life of its own, just like the story of Provincetown's attempt to ban shorts and halter-tops in 1939. In September, after high school principal George Leyden outlined a dress code that excluded "excessively tight clothing" and required students to comb their hair and tuck in their shirts, the *New York Times* dispatched a reporter to take a look at the well-groomed high school.[107]

Student Julia Whorf Kelly, a graduate of the class of 1971, recalled that dress code without fondness. "The teachers would have the girls kneel on the floor after the pledge of allegiance, and if my skirt did not touch the floor when kneeling, I was sent to the principal's office." Sometimes she'd wear a mini skirt to school and get sent home to change.[108]

Yet at the start of the summer of 1966, an open meeting of the board of selectmen was packed as restaurateur Poyant again charged that the town was "seasonally beset by undesirables Mr. Poyant referred to as 'pigs.'" While town officials assured Poyant that everything was under control, Poyant retorted, "Mark my words, we won't have a decent town for long."[109]

You might think that Provincetown residents would learn that the more they decried something, the more publicity they gave it—thereby luring whomever they were trying to repel. Once again, townsfolk managed to catch the attention of the *New York Times*, which dispatched Stephen R. Conn to investigate. The spread on page twenty-nine under the six-column headline "New Pilgrims in Provincetown: Cape Cod Village Is the Site of a 'Beatnik' Beachhead That Is Angering the Local Residents" was completed with three photos. The first showed young people at night lounging at the foot of the World War I monument by town hall. Another, probably taken with a telephoto lens that compressed the crowds to make them look even denser than they were, showed one-way auto traffic fighting its way along the narrow street that it shared with loaded sidewalks of pedestrians and a steady stream of bicyclists, pedestrians and carts under umbrellas. The third photo was of a packed bar at the 140-year-old Crown & Anchor Inn, which "now plays rock 'n' roll" after many years of "cocktail music."

"They're taking our town away from us," the article began, quoting fisherman Manuel Phillips. The article went on to rehash the town-beatnik conflict and also underline one of Provincetown's problems: because tourism had supplanted fishing as the town's main economy, unemployment in the winter of 1965 hit 39.2 percent, with "many residents on welfare." In the summer, in contrast, the unemployment rate was 2.2 percent.[110]

As for the beatniks, "some people still talk about the 13 youths who slept in a chicken house and the youth who slept in an open tomb most of last summer."

Andy Warhol's Explosion Comes to Town

Someone, somewhere, in Provincetown might still have a can of Campbell's Soup signed by Andy Warhol in the manner of his 1962 famous *Campbell's Soup Can* paintings. Warhol and Eric Emerson, "a tall, muscular blond kid" who was part of Warhol's Factory in New York City, went into a grocery store in Provincetown at some point between Wednesday, August 31, and

Andy Warhol saw nothing peculiar about Provincetown. Here, a sand artist sculpts a mermaid as passengers disembark from the *Dolphin VI* whale-watch ship. *Photo by the author.*

Sunday, September 4, 1966, to buy a carton of Marlboro cigarettes and, finding themselves without cash, got the kid at the checkout counter to swap the cigarettes for an autographed soup can.

Warhol and the Velvet Underground, including Lou Reed and Nico, a singer-actress just over from Germany, were in town right before and during Labor Day weekend for "Andy Warhol's Explosion! Exploding Plastic Inevitable," a multimedia road show at the Chrysler Art Museum.[111]

While middle America seemed to find Provincetown bizarre during the summer of '66, Warhol, in contrast, found it a bastion of wholesome American values invaded by his truly freaky entourage of about thirteen: "The silver lamé, leather people in our New York group looked totally alien to the tan, healthy-looking Massachusetts kids." On the beach, Warhol's friends "looked like a giant Clorox spot on the sand, all those pasty-white New York City bodies." One of them wore a leather bikini, but it aroused no interest among the natives.

The toilets stopped up in the houses they rented, and the Velvet Underground began throwing handfuls of excrement out of the windows, according to Warhol. In his *Secret Diaries*, Gerard Malanga, who was among Warhol's entourage, recalled fifteen, including strangers picked up in the streets, staying overnight in one of the rental houses, "wall to wall mattresses."[112]

The shows were performed at 9:00 and 10:30 p.m., with a third show at midnight on Friday in the museum. The police raided one of the shows, Warhol says—the *Advocate* is strangely mute on this weekend event except for advertising it—because the Velvets had stolen leather braids and whips from a "local handicrafts store" that afternoon. "When the police came in, Mary [Woronov] had just strapped Eric to a post and was doing the S&M whipdance around him." The police confiscated the whips and untied Emerson to confiscate his straps.[113]

Shortly before arriving in Provincetown, the Velvets recorded *The Velvet Underground and Nico*, which was released in 1967. The album features songs such as "All Tomorrow's Parties." In 2003, *Rolling Stone* magazine ranked the album as number thirteen of the five hundred greatest albums of all time. Its cover art is a Warhol stick-on banana with a flesh-colored banana beneath it.

FROM BEATNIKS TO HIPPIES, 1960–1969

"Groovin' on a Sunday Afternoon"

And then it was the Summer of Love—the summer of 1967. Carl Feldman advertised a cottage for rent, a "beautiful, knotty pine paneled Cabin situated in gay, natural setting." However, "no hippies or beatniks desired."[114]

Napoleon Eugene Poyant, whose outdoor café and bakery were west of town hall on Commercial Street, couldn't stop peering out his window at the "beatniks, hippies, diggers or whatever they are calling themselves now." As Poyant, whom the *New York Times* described as a "bespectacled Frenchman," stood fuming behind his window, the little groups of hippies were stretched on the lawn, "sleeping, making love not war, admiring each other's long hair, scraggly beards and dirty feet." At night, they loitered on the benches leading to town hall. (Very late in the night, those same benches became a gay cruising spot known as the "meat rack.") Poyant summed it up in a July 20, 1967 letter to the editor as "disgusting foolishness." "Can't somebody do something to stop this?" he asked.

In October, townspeople convened again to discuss what was now out in the open: the hippie problem. Resident Donald Gleason took the long view. "Provincetown's basic problem has existed since the days of O'Neill and Harry Kemp," he said, interestingly invoking a Nobel laureate and a poet who would have a street named after him. "Such people are different by choice. Others come to see the 'characters,'" he said. "Civil disobedience is a big thing right now, with an unpopular war in Vietnam." He did add that the town should not be made a haven for hippies.

John Waters at "Provincetownsend"

Just about that year, 1967, a 1918 Harvard graduate named Prescott Townsend was welcoming "runaways and other gay street youth" to his eccentric home at 1 Bradford Street, "Provincetownsend." Born in 1894, Townsend was one of the first advocates for gay rights and had been summering in Provincetown since the mid-1920s. The film director John Waters, who lived in an apartment in the house, claims in his biography, *Shock Value*, that part of the apartment was constructed from a submarine, and trees grew in the living room.[115] The house burned down around 1970.

Waters first came to Provincetown in 1965, after he was expelled from New York University. In subsequent summers, he clerked in various bookstores, including the one owned by Molly Malone Cook, companion to poet Mary Oliver. He recalled writing six screenplays in Provincetown, including that of his 1972 film *Pink Flamingos*.

Waters said he once saw Judy Garland walking dead drunk down Commercial Street with ten thousand gay men following her like the Pied Piper.[116]

"There Are No Narcotics at Provincetown High"

In a meeting early in December 1967, police chief Francis H. Marshall told the Barnstable County Selectmen's Association at its monthly meeting that Provincetown High was "clean" with respect to narcotics.

"We have a pretty good line on the 'pushers,'" the chief said. The department used plainclothesmen and "imported secret agents to infiltrate the ranks of 'users'" and the "so-called hippie set."[117]

The other chiefs said drugs such as marijuana, LSD, methelin and heroin are "not just something to read about in Greenwich Village, Washington or Boston."

They're here.

One Violent Year: 1968

Grit. Violence. Anger.

The year 1968 was when the horror that had been building through the 1960s came to fruition. On April 4, Martin Luther King Jr. was assassinated. On June 3, Andy Warhol was shot by the deranged Valerie Solanas. On June 6, Robert Kennedy was assassinated in California while campaigning in the Democratic presidential primary.

That was about the year when the head shops opened. One could buy rolling papers, pipes, hookahs, op-art posters, T-shirts and hippie culture stuff. "These shops became hangouts for this new subculture and would take our small, out-of-the-way town into the mainstream of this new pop culture," recalled Julia Whorf Kelly, who was born in 1953 and described herself as a flower child.[118]

To Be-A-Coffee Shop was frequented exclusively by counterculture types and artists. The place served twig tea, and its patrons sat on stuffed couches

The funky Christmas sculpture made of traps and buoys near MacMillan Wharf evokes the town's commercial fishing heritage. *Photo by the author.*

or comfortable chairs. "It was the first alternative coffee shop that the town had known," Kelly said.

By this time, it seemed to some that Provincetown had lost its edge as an art colony. To rectify this, a group of artists, including the poet Stanley Kunitz and painters Robert Motherwell, Philip Malicoat and Salvatore and

Josephine Del Deo, founded the Fine Arts Work Center (FAWC) in the old Days Lumberyard on Pearl Street, which had long rented studio space to artists for nominal sums. Today, FAWC still offers residencies to artists and writers in the early parts of their careers. Generally, 20 are chosen from over 1,100 applicants worldwide.[119]

A Holdover from Another Time

Rear Admiral Donald B. MacMillan, the last survivor of the 1909 Robert E. Peary expedition, which reached the North Pole, received a telegram of congratulations on his ninety-fourth birthday from President-elect Richard M. Nixon.[120] In 1957, MacMillan Wharf had been named after him.

A few months later, a reporter from the *New York Times* visited MacMillan's house on Commercial Street to interview him on the sixtieth anniversary of his expedition to the North Pole. Although MacMillan never set foot on the North Pole because frozen feet compelled him to drop out of the "final push," Nixon again sent MacMillan a message as yet another frontier was about to be broken: Apollo 11 astronauts were scheduled to land on the moon.

MacMillan, a veteran of twenty-seven expeditions to the Arctic, was "still erect as a stanchion on a schooner's fo'c'sle," the reporter noted. The first-floor porch of his "shipshape home" served as his deck, and he paced it daily. While MacMillan's "deep blue eyes are clouded by glaucoma and cataracts," he cocks his head toward the Atlantic.

His wife, Miriam, who was just four when the North Pole was discovered, accompanied MacMillan on nine expeditions. When asked why he remained a bachelor to age sixty, MacMillan replied, "Just never had the time before."

"He Digs Girls"

Apollo 11 astronauts landed on the moon on July 20, 1969, but that might have been the only good news of the summer. On June 22, Judy Garland died, apparently of an overdose of barbiturates. On July 18, Mary Jo Kopechne died, a victim of Senator Ted Kennedy's wild driving in Chappaquiddick. More horror was to come on August 9, when Charles Manson and his deranged cult followers murdered the pregnant actress Sharon Tate and her friends in her Los Angeles home.

Norman Mailer wrote that he "hated his beloved Provincetown this summer above all."[121] While it seemed that most people were stoned on marijuana, drinking parties went on for twelve hours. Mailer, who won the Pulitzer Prize for nonfiction for *The Armies of the Night* that year, dubbed Provincetown "the Wild West of the East." The town was downright dangerous. In fact, it was reeling from the revelations that had begun in March in the nearby woods of Truro.

In January, serial killer Antone Charles "Tony" Costa, twenty-four, was living in a guesthouse operated by Patricia Morton at 5 Standish Street. In the spring, the first dismembered bodies were dug up in the woods of Truro.

Costa's victims were not famous. Some of the suspected seven young women he killed were caught up in the hippie drug scene. Others were merely young women on vacation. Take Patricia Walsh and Mary Anne Wysocki, two twenty-three-year-olds from Providence, Rhode Island, who drove to Provincetown for a weekend winter getaway. Walsh was a second grade teacher, and Wysocki was a student at Rhode Island College. On the afternoon of Friday, January 24, the pair arrived at the small Victorian guesthouse and inquired about a room. Morton had one room available, and the pair paid twenty-four dollars for the two nights. Morton took them on a tour of the house and along the way introduced them to Costa, who was already a divorced father of three. Originally from Somerville, he came to Provincetown to finish high school after he was convicted of assault and attempted rape of a fourteen-year-old neighborhood girl when he was seventeen. He graduated from Provincetown High School in 1962 and married fourteen-year-old Avis Johnson. Since graduation, he had worked as a part-time carpenter, electrician and drug dealer. He also operated as a snitch for the Provincetown Police Department.[122]

Walsh and Wysocki disappeared during the weekend, along with Walsh's blue VW bug, which was seen first in the woods where the bodies would be found and later turned up in Burlington, Vermont. Costa told a number of tales about the pair, including that they had taken off for California after selling him Walsh's car. When three dismembered bodies were found in shallow graves "in the sand dunes of the Cape Cod National Seashore," the story made the *New York Times*, and this was no longer a local story about two possible runaways.[123] With the discovery of three bodies, this was now the story of a serial killer.

Dr. Daniel Hiebert, now age seventy-nine, acting in his capacity as medical examiner, examined the first body dug up in the woods. Hiebert was "tall, stooped, with watery blue eyes behind thick spectacles." Because the corpse was missing some teeth, Hiebert said it was that of a white female aged fifty to sixty. It was in fact that of a nineteen-year-old.[124]

As might happen only in a small, somewhat isolated town, Hiebert reappears many times in this story. In an interview Hiebert gave to a *Boston Globe* reporter a couple of days after Costa was arrested in Boston on March 6, he said he had delivered Costa's mother, mother-in-law and wife. He apparently prescribed Costa tranquilizers after one of Costa's interviews with police and also gave Costa's mother tranquilizers. The headline on the article was "Medical Examiner is Costa's Doctor."[125]

Provincetown's unique grittiness was evident. "Hostile to outsiders, enclosed within itself, distinct, separate from the prim and orderly charm of the rest of Cape Cod, Provincetown was an outpost of singularity, a frontier unconnected with the rest of Cape Cod." Worse, the "freaks"—that is, members of the authority-hating, drug-using counterculture—loved Costa.[126] It is painful now to look at newspaper pictures of teenage girls smiling and waving to Costa outside the courthouse. Either these girls—who could easily have been Costa's next victims—believed he did not commit the crimes or they admired him for committing the crimes.

Not all young people felt comfortable around Costa. "There was one man who stood out as different, though. I never liked him and thought him 'odd.' He would talk to us and invite us to his apartment," Julia Whorf Kelly recalled. "We would visit him at his apartment after school and smoke cigarettes and sometimes pot. He asked us once if we wanted to come into the woods nearby and see his 'magical garden.'" Costa's garden, where he cultivated marijuana, was where he buried his victims.

Kelly knew one of Costa's local victims, whom Costa apparently picked up while she was hitchhiking. Her body was found in a duffel bag. "I was subpoenaed to testify at his trial and face him on the stand and to identify the duffel bag the poor girl was found in," she wrote.

While psychiatrists called Costa a "schizoid personality" and "a modern-day Marquis de Sade," district attorney Edmund Dinis turned the case into a media firestorm by saying, falsely, that the hearts of each girl had been removed and teeth marks found on the bodies. When a reporter asked if this was the work of a "Cape Cod vampire," Dinis nodded.

"The press is bad," Provincetown police chief Francis Marshall said, "but the tourists are even worse." People arrived in town with shovels, intent on digging in the Truro woods to see if they might find another body. (The spot is said to draw sightseers to this day.) It was on the wall of a Truro Laundromat that the following words were scrawled: "Tony Costa digs girls."[127]

In the months before Costa's trial, "he was the most famous American then accused of mass murder," Kurt Vonnegut noted in his 1974 book of essays, *Wampeters Foma & Granfalloons*. When Manson and his cultists were arrested in August 1969, after murdering actress Sharon Tate and her friends, "Costa himself ceased to be a celebrity—became overnight what he had been in the beginning, a nobody."[128]

It wasn't until a year later that Costa was brought to trial in superior court, charged with the murders of Walsh and Wysocki. The pair had been shot in the heads, raped and cut up into seven parts. Costa's four-man defense team planned to try to prove that Costa was "under the domination and the intoxication of mind-altering drugs," including marijuana, hashish, amphetamines, heroin, barbiturates, LSD and morphine.[129]

"Everybody closely related to the case has had some experience with drugs," an investigator for the defense told Vonnegut. When Vonnegut himself asked some young people familiar with the "Provincetown drug scene" which drug Costa might have been high on when he killed his victims, the answer was always "speed."[130] Chillingly, Vonnegut's daughter Edith knew Costa from her summer studying art in Provincetown.

The jury convicted Costa on May 22 of first-degree murder, apparently not buying the drug theory. Costa was remanded to the Massachusetts Correctional Institute at Walpole to serve two concurrent life sentences. In November 1971, his bid for acquittal or conviction of a lesser sentence was turned down. In May 1974, he hanged himself with his belt. He was buried in Provincetown in an unmarked grave next to his mother.

Elsewhere, in Greenwich Village—

While Provincetown was preoccupied with the doings of its own serial killer that summer, something of import happened in Provincetown's unofficial "sister city," Greenwich Village. On June 28, 1969, what would be known later as the Stonewall Riots at 53 Christopher Street took place between 1:00 and 4:00 a.m.

The Stonewall Inn was a gay bar that catered to drag queens and others. When police arrived to arrest bar patrons at about 1:00 a.m., the patrons, instead of going quietly, rioted. The event, now heralded as the beginning of the LGBT movement, reverberated in later decades throughout the gay world and in Provincetown.

"There are times when you just know the rules've been changed," says Franny, a drag queen in John Preston's 1983 novel, *Franny: The Queen of Provincetown*. Franny, who was in Provincetown when he learned about the riot, was by this time middle aged. "There wasn't anything immediate going to happen... I certainly was willing to wait a few more years. 'Cause things had to be different now."[131]

4
A Decade of Change,
1970-1979

Everyone who lives here is blessed.
—Alice Brock of Provincetown

Nancy Whorf and *L'heure Bleu*

L'heure bleu is what the French call that brief period between sunset and darkness. Jacques Guerlain, the great early twentieth century *parfumier*, called this "that uncertain hour" and named a perfume after it. *L'heure bleu*—really much less than an hour in length in the winter—is a magical time when even the snow on the streets might turn blue. Streaks of orange from the just-set sun might stain the western sky.

Nancy Whorf has painted that moment in many of her large oils.

Whorf, who was born in 1930, lived in Provincetown almost all her life. A daughter of the famous watercolorist John Whorf, Whorf had her first painting lessons when she was five or six. She'd go up into her father's attic studio, where he painted on a slanting table, standing up. Later, as teenagers, both she and her sister Carol painted furniture for the decorator Peter Hunt. Their next-door neighbor, Wendy Hackett Everett, whose mother, Mary "Bubs" Hackett, was also an artist, remembered that they worked for Hunt after school, all day on Saturday and during the summers when they were seventeen and eighteen.[132]

The Whorf family plot is in Provincetown Cemetery. Watercolorist John Whorf and his daughter Nancy Whorf Kelly represent two generations of talent in this multigenerational artist family. *Photo by the author.*

Although Everett and Carol Whorf Westcott left Provincetown when they married, Whorf, after leaving briefly, returned after her divorce with her three daughters, Megan, Julia and Lydia Kelly. She entered into a romantic dalliance with Herman Tasha—the husband of Sunny Tasha, who would later build the poet Kemp his house—that lasted until Herman Tasha's death. She continued decorating folk art furniture, which she sold in Wellfleet until the late 1980s, when she turned to easel work. Known as a colorist, Whorf painted with a palette knife so as not to get caught up in detail. Her canvases are large—sometimes three by four feet—and she evoked Provincetown's light and mood in paintings such as *Winter-Commercial Street.* "As long as you feel you have something to say, you keep painting," she once said.

Whorf and her daughters lived the life of bohemians, with money coming in irregularly. Her middle daughter, Julia Kelly, published a charming reminiscence of that household called *Feast or Famine: Growing Up Bohemian in Provincetown.* God help the artist or writer living in Provincetown who didn't like fish. "Most of the time...our mainstay meal was fish; it was inexpensive and often free." One time, an anonymous fisherman dropped three hundred pounds of bluefish in Whorf's yard. Whorf was as creative as possible in preparing the strongly flavored fish, but bluefish is bluefish. Eventually, "anything cooked in the black iron fry pan, however, tasted like bluefish. Pork chops, eggs, pancakes, no matter, they all had that hidden secret flavor…bluefish."[133] At one point, Herman Tasha made "skully-jo," a Provincetown specialty, right in the house. The *Advocate* shared the secrets of skully-jo in September 1937: First, you clean the fish and cut off its head. Then you cure the fish in brine or dry salt and hang it out to dry for weeks and weeks in the salty wind, "making it nearly as hard as the Cap'n's walking stick." Some aficionados kept the petrified fish in their pockets and gnawed on it when they felt peaked.

One might note that the *Advocate* assumed a person engaged in making skully-jo would dry the fish outdoors, not in an upstairs hall and attic. "For several weeks I had to duck under the stiff cardboard-like fish to get to bed. Everything I wore smelled like fish, everything I ate tasted like fish," Kelly remembered.[134]

In *Sledding at Dinner Time*, the sky beyond the leafless branches is a fiery orange-yellow. But the snow in the shadowy spaces behind the buildings has turned a purple-blue-gray. And in *Late Afternoon in Winter*, again the sky at the horizon is a bright streak of yellow-white that is staining the fronts of buildings orange. The asphalt road, like the high sky, is purple.

Both paintings are scenes of Provincetown with a steeple peeping up in the distance.

The light is key in *Race Point Station*. The sandy path and the sand dunes are blue—a deeper blue than the sky. A dog and a man carrying what is perhaps a rifle are walking the path. It could be just before dawn but is more probably dusk.

"Painting mostly with a palette knife on Masonite board, her paintings became a vehicle for expressing not only her unique vision of her beloved home and town, but also allowed her to develop her perception of color, light, and compositional movement," Kelly wrote.[135] Whorf died in 2009 at the age of seventy-nine. Her work, and the work of many other Provincetown master artists, is represented by the Berta Walker Gallery at 208 Bradford Street.

The '60s Were Not Over Yet

In 1971, as the war in Vietnam dragged on, the counterculture thrived. If 1968 had been a watershed year for student protestors and discontent, not much had improved. The *New York Times* covered a Provincetown town

Love 'n' Happiness. The Little Store, a landmark at 227 Commercial Street since 1971, closed in November 2011, when owners Eddie and Judy Polay retired after forty years. *Detail of painting by Andrea Sawyer.*

meeting in March 1971. The problem now was that, while in the summer the town of 4,100 year-round residents swelled to about 20,000 residents, at the end of the summer of '71 about 600 "of the long-haired young people stayed to weather the Cape Cod winter." And they registered to vote at age nineteen.[136] By March 8, 570 new voters had been added to the 2,100 already on the rolls, and of these, nearly 500 were young people. Of these, about 110 also went on welfare over the winter.

"The once thriving fishing industry now keeps only about 30 boats sporadically occupied," the *New York Times* reported, adding in a gloomy way that the town's "primacy as an arts center" was over.

One of the newcomers was John Short, twenty-three, an associate editor of the *Harvard Crimson* in 1970. Accentuating the generation gap was the *Times* reporter's emphasis on Short's hair, a "head of billowing-curls like a huge brown chrysanthemum." Short and two others took over the *Advocate*, which they changed from a "local chatterbox" to a hometown newspaper reporting town politics and business. That year's town meeting attracted nine hundred instead of the usual four hundred. Over two hundred "long-haired women and bearded men" sat in the balcony. They all went out to Pilgrim Club later that night to dance. They wore beads and leather and danced to "loud, raucous music."

How the young newcomers might legally, through their voice at town meeting, change the future of the town remained to be seen.

"Take Me to the Monument on Time!"

Before 9:00 a.m. on July 21, 1972, two twenty-three-year-olds from California were wed on the observation deck of the Pilgrim Monument, the *Cape Cod Standard-Times* reported.[137]

"At first we were going to get married on the beach, but every hippie was doing that," the groom told the newspaper. "It was really something bizarre, like out of a Fellini movie. It felt like a castle."

So why not get married in the monument? Why not climb the 116 steps and sixty ramps to the top of the 252-foot granite tower?

Not surprisingly, no official wanted to climb up the monument to perform the ceremony. The town clerk said he had vertigo. The couple finally found someone who complied, and history was made.

The Arts in Truro

Something of the arts world moved to an old barn in the dunes of Truro that summer when Joyce Johnson and others opened the Truro Center for the Arts at Castle Hill. Johnson, a writer and sculptor, had been teaching from her home. Castle Hill, as it is called, proved to be a magnet for the art and literary crowd. Through the decades, many names associated with Provincetown have taught there.[138]

The '60s Draw to an End

The year 1973 "marked the true end, too, of one of the most turbulent decades in American history, the sixties."[139]

When the Vietnam War ended in April, the leaders of the counterculture "fell off the radar screen." The Watergate Hearings were televised all

The names of ninety-six Vietnam War veterans are etched in the war monument alongside the names of veterans from World War II, Korea and other wars. *Photo by the author.*

through the summer of '73. Just as novelist Willa Cather had written, over fifty years before, that "the world broke in two in 1922 or thereabouts," so in 1973, "it seemed to many Americans that history itself had become unhinged from any master narrative or enterprise with a secure outcome."[140]

In Provincetown, the names of ninety-six Vietnam War veterans were etched into the war monument.

A Paean to Portuguese Cookery

That same year, 1973, the future celebrity chef and author Anthony Bourdain, age eighteen, breezed into Provincetown and got a job as a dishwasher at a restaurant he calls "the Dreadnaught." (Much speculation has gone on over the real name of the Dreadnaught. Bourdain has admitted, without quite saying it, that it was the Flagship.) The Dreadnaught was "a big, old, ramshackle driftwood pile, built out over the water on ancient wooden pylons." The décor included "hanging fishnets, hurricane lamps, buoys, nautical bric-a-brac, the bars fashioned from halved lifeboats."[141]

In the early 1970s, Bourdain tells us in *Kitchen Confidential*, there was no culinary culture. "Most fish in P-town was slapped boneless and skinless onto sizzle-platters, drizzled with clarified butter and paprika and then broiled to death."[142] "Mario's Restaurant" (aka Ciro & Sal's) was "fairly sophisticated stuff for the time."

Ciro & Sal's opened in the early 1950s. Ciro Cozzi and Sal Del Deo were both artists studying under Henry Hensche. Their first restaurant was a pizza parlor in the dirt-floored basement of Cozzi's house in Peter Hunt Alley. Not too long after opening, they paved the dirt floor and began serving dinner. Alice Brock, of Alice's Restaurant fame, ate her first solo dinner as a teenager at Ciro & Sal's and later, as an adult, relived it. Amazingly, her second dinner came up to the expectations left by that first "ultimate experience." "After dinner I was in seventh heaven, a bit crocked, and I sent a note down to the kitchen. I don't remember now the exact wording, but it was a love note," she recalled in *My Life as a Restaurant*.

An appendix to *Ciro & Sal's Cookbook* lists the names of 206 "influential personalities who have passed through the restaurant's doors." Beginning with Truman Capote, the astonishing list includes John Wayne, writer Annie Dillard and members of the Boston Bruins hockey team. "Hans Hofmann always complained that there was not enough color in the dishes," we learn.

Ciro & Sal's opened in the 1950s on what was Peter Hunt Alley. The restaurant is still going strong on what is now called Kiley Court, just off Commercial Street in the East End. *Photo by the author.*

In a small town such as Provincetown, awkward moments could occur in restaurants. "Over the years, the hostesses at both of Ciro's restaurants in Provincetown had had to be very careful never to seat Norman next to any of his ex-wives," the *Ciro's & Sal's Cookbook* informs us.[196]

Eventually, Bourdain met Howard Mitcham, the sole "name chef in town." "Though drunk most of the time, and difficult to understand, Howard was a revered elder statesman of Cape Cod cookery," Bourdain wrote.[143]

Mitcham, born in 1917 in Mississippi, once owned an art gallery in Greenwich Village. He was deaf. Through the years, Mitcham cooked in many Provincetown restaurants, in particular Pepe's Wharf, on Commercial Street, as he divided his year between Provincetown and New Orleans. Beginning in 1965, he also wrote a food column in the *Advocate* called "Cape Tip Gourmet." His *Provincetown Seafood Cookbook* sprang from these columns. Mitcham went on to write six books of cookery and reminiscence before he died in Hyannis in 1996.

Mitcham "was the first chef I knew to appreciate fully the local Portagee cuisine: the spicy cumin-scented squid stews, the linguica-laden kale soups, the coupling of fish and pork sausages," Bourdain wrote. "Howard showed us that there was hope for us as cooks. That food could be a calling."[144]

Mitcham's *Provincetown Seafood Cookbook* begins with a paean to Portuguese cuisine. He explains the marinade *vinha d'albos*, or "wine of garlic." This concoction is "the beautiful spicy garlicky marinade which makes Portuguese food seem like witchcraft or black magic." Amazingly, before refrigeration,

Mitcham says, you could keep a fish fresh floating in *vinha d'albos* for several days. He also recommends a dish of Portuguese squid stew, although, he warns, "it's not a dish for John Q. Public."

Bourdain recalled Mitcham's annual clambake in memory of his fisherman friend John J. Gaspie. They dug pits in the sand, buried coals and lowered trashcans into the holes. Soon the trashcans were filled with quahogs, lobsters, codfish, vegetables, potatoes and corn cooking "while everyone drank themselves silly."

The Lady in the Dunes

It's always a dog walker who makes the gruesome discoveries. Usually it's in the early morning, while others are asleep, that the dog walker lets the dog off the leash. Free at last, the dog romps, sometimes straying too far into the woods, into the dunes.

Dogs like to explore. They like things that smell.

In this case, it was a hot afternoon when a thirteen-year-old girl went looking for her beagle in the dunes of the Cape Cod National Seashore at Race Point. She heard her pet barking and found him sniffing at what appeared to be a sunbather. So it was that the young girl discovered the "lady in the dunes," the victim of a grotesque murder.[145] That was July 26, 1974, and the murder remains unsolved to this day.

The woman's remains were lying about a mile east of the Race Point Ranger Station. She had been dead for a week to ten days, and she was nude, recumbent on a light green, heavy cotton beach blanket with her head resting on her folded jeans. Her hands were missing and the left side of her skull crushed. Her head was nearly severed from her neck.

Teams of police and a bloodhound scoured the dunes for clues. They came up with nothing. On October 19, the woman was buried in St. Peter's Cemetery under a stone marked "Unidentified Female Body Found Race Point Dunes." Her nearest and dearest did not attend the ceremony. She was exhumed in 2000, and today her skull is stored in a state police crime lab; in May 2010, a new composite sculpture was made of her head in the hopes that someone would be able to identify her. No one has come forward.

The "lady in the dunes," as she has been called now for four decades, had long auburn or reddish-blond hair and an athletic build. When she was found, her hair was bound in a ponytail. Her toenails were painted pink. She stood five feet, six and a half inches tall, weighed 145 pounds and her age was estimated at between twenty and forty. The best clue the investigators had was her $5,000 worth of dental work, including several gold inlays. Police mailed her dental chart to five thousand Massachusetts dentists, to dental societies in forty-nine states and to law enforcement agencies in the United States, Canada and Europe. No one made a match.

The most poignant part of the case is that apparently no one missed the woman.

Yet "some family has to be missing a loved one somewhere," James J. Meads, the Provincetown officer in charge of the case, said in a 1983 interview. "And they have never come forward and that disturbs me. I think about that a lot."[146]

The Provincetown Police anonymous tip line remains open at 508-487-2828.

Provincetown Business Guild

In 1977, a group of artists, intent on revitalizing Provincetown as an art colony, founded the Long Point Gallery on Commercial Street in the East End. An artists' cooperative, it thrived for twenty years.

While through the 1960s the "generation gap" in the form of roving bands of hippies was paramount in articles about Provincetown, by 1978, the town's gay aspect was back on the front burner.

In a radical change from just about a decade earlier, when gay businesses were maligned, in 1978 the nonprofit Provincetown Business Guild was formed to promote gay tourism and business. In the beginning, the group had twenty members. When, the following year, one of them pitched an article on Provincetown to *After Dark* magazine, nationwide recognition of Provincetown as a gay destination resulted.[147] Today, the group "helps maintain the #1 Gay Community in America by promoting Provincetown to the LGBT market worldwide," according to its website.

Norman Mailer: Alive and Well in Provincetown

In 1979, Norman Mailer's Provincetown house at 565 Commercial Street went up for public auction. This was a house with a long literary pedigree that included ownership by John Dos Passos. At issue was the $80,000 in

Norman Mailer's fourth wife, Beverly Bentley Mailer, was still living at 565 Commercial Street when the family home was sold in a tax auction as a part of their divorce. The couple had bought the house in 1966. *Photo by the author.*

back taxes and penalties that Mailer had accrued by not filing tax returns in 1976 and 1977. Mailer had bought the house for $60,000 in 1966, and this is the price the IRS sold it for. Mailer's soon-to-be ex-fourth-wife Beverly Bentley Mailer was seeking the deed to the house, as well as $1,000 a week alimony, contending that she had lived there for thirteen years and raised Norman's two sons there. The divorce proceedings were messy, and even after the house was auctioned off, Beverly Mailer refused to move. In 1981, Judge Robert A. Welsh in District Court, Orleans, ordered her out of house. He also ordered her to reimburse the current owners $13,650 in back rent.[148]

5
New Threats,
1980-1999

Provincetown possesses, has always possessed, a steady, grieving competence in the face
of all that can happen to people. It watches and waits; it keeps the lights burning.
—Michael Cunningham, Land's End

Compassion in the Age of AIDS

If we are born, we must die. This is the natural order of things.

What is not natural is for children to die before their parents, for young men in their twenties, thirties and forties to die in the hundreds from a disease. This was the look of the AIDS crisis of the 1980s and '90s.

While gay America had made strides toward recognition during the decade since the Stonewall Riots, something ominous lay on the horizon. It began with sporadic reports in the newspapers during the spring of 1981. The official first reference to the new disease came on June 5, 1981, in a Centers for Disease Control and Prevention report on a rare lung infection afflicting five young gay men in Los Angeles.[149] "The Gay Cancer," it was first called in headlines. In 1982, it would be called acquired immune deficiency syndrome or, simply, AIDS.

Like the Spanish influenza of 1918 that killed men and women in their prime, AIDS in the 1980s and 1990s killed previously healthy people, largely gay men, in the prime of their lives. While the influenza epidemic spread fast and killed fast, a patient suffering from AIDS could linger for months or years.

In the beginning, rumors abounded about how AIDS was spread. Shared drinking glasses, doorknobs, French kissing, sneezing, mosquito bites—all were suspect. While at-risk groups were first defined as homosexuals, IV-drug users, Haitians and hemophiliacs—which led to making pariahs of those people—later it was declared that everyone was equally susceptible. "It's not who you are, it's what you do," said one federal public health campaign in 1988. Those with AIDS were evicted from housing, not allowed to attend school and even refused medical care in those early days.

By June 1983, there were 1,601 cases of AIDS nationwide. And the fear was growing. Provincetown's business community worried that misinformation on AIDS would drive vacationers away as surely as gas shortages, red tides and hurricanes had done in the past.[150]

That same month, when Provincetown's police were issued rubber gloves to wear when handling AIDS patients, Boston TV stations WNEV and WBZ

This moody painting of the Pilgrim Monument in fog evokes the shadow that hung over the town in the early, heartbreaking days of the AIDS crisis. *Painting by Oris Folsom.*

played it up. Those were the days before dentists and healthcare workers routinely wore gloves. Gloves and masks represented something new and frightening: the thought that AIDS could infect anyone, that you didn't have to engage in gay sex acts to contract AIDS.

"Before and after," Randy Shilts wrote in *And the Band Played On*.[151] "The epidemic would cleave lives in two, the way a great war or depression presents a commonly understood point of reference around which an entire society defines itself."[152]

Yet that summer of 1983, the tourist trade was good. Preston Babbitt was president of the Provincetown Business Guild, a group of 130 gay establishments. Harold Goodstein was president of the 300-member Provincetown Chamber of Commerce. During a hot summer weekend, Provincetown's population might swell to eighty thousand, counting day-trippers and weekenders.

When people look back now at that time of AIDS in Provincetown, they mention how proud they are at how well the town rose to meet the crisis. In 1983, town nurse Alice Foley and others founded the Provincetown AIDS Support Group. With Babbitt, who owned the Rose & Crown Guest House, Foley made her rounds tending the desperately ill. Because of the disease's stigma, she parked up the street from the homes of her patients. The support group also distributed information and encouraged businesses to install condom machines in restrooms.

Foley was born in Cambridge in 1932, trained as a nurse and moved to Provincetown in about 1970 so she could live openly as a gay woman. She worked various jobs outside of her field but finally moved back into nursing when she began working at the Drop-In Center set up to help young people with drug problems and sexually transmitted diseases.[153] Appointed the town nurse in 1980—essentially the town's director of health—she stepped up to the bat before AIDS even had a name. People who remembered her after she died in 2009 recalled a woman who could be abrasive but was a hardworking, fearless pioneer in the days when little was known about AIDS.[154]

"No one died alone," Foley said in an oral history called *There Were Ghosts Everywhere: An Oral History of AIDS in Provincetown*. "It became almost family-like between volunteers and clients."[155]

By 1984, there were four known cases of AIDS in Provincetown, and by 1987, there were twenty-five cases. In 1985, Rock Hudson died of AIDS, and the world put a face on the disease. Two years later, Liberace also died of AIDS, and two years after that, the photographer Robert Mapplethorpe passed. In 1985 or 1986, Foley said, AIDS patients from the cities began selling out and buying property in Provincetown to live their final days among sympathetic gay people.

In August 1987, there was a "new seriousness" in a town that loved a party more than anything. At the Boatslip Resort, participants in the 4:00 p.m. tea dances on the deck filled a large glass with one-dollar bills for the AIDS support group. Fear still ran rampant. The manager of the Post Office Café said one customer refused to drink a beer that had been poured into a glass, "but I think she was just homophobic, anyway."[156]

In 1988, AIDS cases in Provincetown rose to forty, giving Provincetown the highest per capita number of cases in the state. Residents and visitors had by now donated $150,000 to care for the stricken. Over forty volunteers worked with Foley and Community Care director Doreen Devlin.[157] In May, the town hosted its first AIDS conference, and in October, the Lamplighter Living Center group home for persons with AIDS opened.

"We have a cloud over us—the Big A," a business owner said. "Now if there's a clique of twenty and four die, well, then you don't feel so groovy."

AIDS moved through the gay population indiscriminately. A year later, among the dead were Chuck L. Vetter, a handyman at Spiritus Pizza Shop, age forty-one; William E. Schafer Jr., age thirty-one, a cook and artist; Edmond J. DiStasi, fifty-three, owner of the Front Street Restaurant; and Jon Perry, forty-three, who taught expository writing at Harvard. By the end of the 1980s, 100,000 people in the United States suffered from AIDS, and by 1992, AIDS was the number one cause of death for U.S. men ages twenty-five to forty-four.[158]

"Julian kept hearing that someone else had got it, was living with it, was fighting it, was failing, reviving, dying or dead of it," R.D. Skillings wrote in his novel of the AIDS years in Provincetown, *How Many Die*.[159]

AIDS in Provincetown was different from AIDS in, say, Boston. It was up close and personal. Because the town's year-round population was only 3,500, working with persons with AIDS in Provincetown was unlike working with AIDS patients in a big city. These were the people you saw at the post office, your co-workers, your neighbors.

"On the street, reft of the summer multitude, the sick stood out starkly, spectral pairs of slowly moving men, one helping, the other emaciated, muffled up in scarves and overcoat, hollow-eyed, stubble-bearded, inward-gazing," Skillings wrote.

"This just encompassed your whole life," said Irene Rabinowitz, who had also worked with AIDS patients in New York. Rabinowitz later became the head of Helping Our Women (HOW). "It became overwhelming just because of the intimacy of the size of the community."

Between 1983 and 1995, 228 residents of Provincetown died of AIDS.[160] With funerals and memorial services almost every weekend, there was no time to grieve.

"Ghosts were everywhere in town in the early '90s," an AIDS volunteer recalled. "The whole town felt haunted for a while."

She spoke of the disjointedness of being present at the death of a patient, watching as he was pronounced dead, watching him zipped into a body bag and then walking out into the blazing sunshine of Commercial Street, where tourists were eating ice cream.

"You lose all your friends," another volunteer said. "You have to find new friends, form a new family."

"Provincetown has been widowed by the AIDS epidemic," Michael Cunningham wrote.

In 1993, Foley left her position with the town and became executive director of the Provincetown AIDS Support Group.

Finally, in 1996, for the first time, the number of new cases of AIDS declined. That same year, Foley House opened at 214 Bradford Street. The rebuilt house has ten units of housing and a common living space for persons with AIDS or HIV. As the millennium approached, new drugs called protease inhibitors began to prevent the symptoms of full-blown AIDS in people who tested positive for the HIV virus.

Thirty years after the AIDS crisis began, the needs of HIV-positive people are different than they were in the days when Foley ministered to them out of her car. Provincetown still responds to AIDS by hosting fundraising events such as the Provincetown 5k Walk and Run in July for the AIDS Support Group of Cape Cod. Foley died in her sleep of heart failure on April 19, 2009. She was seventy-six.

"This crazy town," a character says in *How Many Die*. "I keep telling myself to go live in some normal place like Florida. But every time I go away I realize it's hell out there. We're lucky to have this lunatic asylum to come back to."

"Well. When you consider. The blighted lives. The people who were able to bloom here and nowhere else. I owe my life to this town," his friend responds.

Norman Mailer Moves to 627 Commercial Street

In the midst of this sad time, Norman and his sixth wife, Norris Church Mailer, debated, at the dinner table, if they should pour "a line of lime" between the Mailers' new house at 627 Commercial Street and the residence of their next-door neighbor, a gay man who apparently had AIDS. Their idea was that the lime would "stop the spread of AIDS."[161] The fear factor generated by AIDS was very high in the early 1980s, even among educated people.

Mailer had managed to buy his big brick East End house with the help of Roy Cohn, who denied he was dying of AIDS. Cohn, the notorious sidekick of Senator Joe McCarthy, never acknowledged that he was gay and would die of AIDS on August 2, 1986, at age fifty-nine.

Cohn had risen to prominence during the Army-McCarthy hearings televised for thirty-six days between April and June 1954. To hear McCarthy tell it, Communists were under every bush. In Provincetown, the *Advocate*'s letters to the editor had reflected the world at large, with some applauding McCarthy and others deriding him. Cohn was just twenty-seven when he came to Brewster in August 1954 to address a crowd of over five hundred from all over the Cape. His topic: "The Menace of Communism." Cohn warned his audience that twenty-five to thirty-five thousand Communists were currently operating in the United States. During the three decades following the hearings, Cohn had remained controversial and was often alleged to be a "mob lawyer."

In her excellent biography of Mailer, Mary V. Dearborn explicates the bizarre circumstances under which Mailer bought 627 Commercial and then rented the renovated garage (or boathouse, as it is sometimes called) at 625 Commercial to Cohn. Mailer was already well acquainted with the particular East End neighborhood, as it was just down from his old house at 565 Commercial.

Through a series of complex financial arrangements, Mailer and his wife bought the property jointly with writer Peter Manso. Cohn became a silent third in the agreement, bringing funding to the table for Mailer, whose tangled finances made it nearly impossible for him to obtain a conventional mortgage. In the spring of 1984, the Mailers moved into half of the house, with Manso and his companion, Ellen Hawkes, moving into the other half. Cohn moved into the renovated garage in early 1985. Although Cohn paid rent, Mailer did not want to be associated with Cohn publicly. "Once America's most macho novelist, Norman now had for a 'tenant' (and secret benefactor) a floridly gay pasha with an entourage of young men."[162] After Cohn's death, the waterfront property, which is a "freestanding condominium," was sold and renovated.[163]

The house shared by Norman and Norris Church Mailer at 627 Commercial Street was for sale at $3.5 million in the winter of 2014. The Mailers moved into the house in 1984. *Photo by the author.*

Meanwhile, the relationship deteriorated between the Mailers and Manso, who had "idolized Norman since he was a teenager" and written his doctoral thesis at Berkeley on Mailer's work.[164] At the end of the summer of 1985, Manso and Hawkes moved out. In 1987, Manso published *Mailer: His Life and Times.*

Mailer lived at 627 Commercial Street from 1990 to his death in 2007. His third-floor study was used in the film of his Provincetown novel *Tough Guys Don't Dance.*

"I loved that house," Norris Church Mailer wrote in her 2010 memoir, *A Ticket to the Circus.* "It was big enough for all of us—five bedrooms and four and a half bathrooms, with Norman and me splitting the attic floor for our offices."

In 2008, the house became home to the Norman Mailer Center and Writers Colony. The nonprofit group was unable to raise sufficient funds to purchase the house. As of March 2014, the house was on the market with a price tag of $3.5 million.

The Town Crier Goes Rogue

The restaurateur Eugene Napoleon Poyant, hater of hippies and other degenerate "pigs" back in the late 1960s, resurfaced in 1983 clad in the costume of the town crier. His job was to stroll among the tourists near MacMillan Wharf, talking about Provincetown's history as a fishing village and gently steering tourists into art galleries.

In 1987, though, at the age of sixty-six, Poyant made headlines for revisiting his crusading days. He allegedly said gays, lesbians and the devil himself had taken over the Universalist Church. And instead of aiding local businesses, he steered tourists away from restaurants he believed were staffed with gay waiters.

Although Poyant, who had lived in Provincetown for forty-two years, denied the charges, the board of selectmen voted unanimously to strip Poyant of any official badges or emblems identifying him as an official town crier.[165]

Trial by Fire

As the 1980s merged into the 1990s, rough times continued in Provincetown. Provincetown has always been particularly wary of fires. Firefighting in Provincetown is made difficult by the many large wooden buildings set close together; cars and other obstructions in the narrow streets; the summer crowds; extreme weather; and the town's remote location. Help from other towns is not at hand. (And the town has, as well, spawned elusive and persistent arsonists, notably during the Great Depression and just after the millennium.) Provincetown established its fire department in 1836, making it the oldest department on Cape Cod.

The 1990s were a particularly fiery decade. On October 29, 1990, the three-story Pilgrim House at 336 Commercial Street, possibly built as early as 1781, was destroyed by a suspicious fire in a four-alarm blaze. Henry David Thoreau slept in the Pilgrim House during his 1857 walk around Cape Cod. Seven buildings were damaged or destroyed. Fourteen civilians and firefighters were injured.[166]

The following year, on April 17, 1991, fire damaged the Atlantic House, which had been damaged by a previous fire in 1978.

On November 14, 1996, one woman was killed and dozens evacuated from the Maushop Elderly Housing Complex in a three alarm-fire at 2:30 a.m.

On February 10, 1998, a five-alarm blaze broke out in one of the largest fires in Cape history. Destroyed were Whaler's Wharf complex, the Crown & Anchor Inn, Handcrafters and Marine Specialties buildings. The venerable Crown & Anchor at 247 Commercial Street was where Bobby Short had performed nightly in July and August 1962. Thirty-nine departments from two counties were activated as the dramatic fire threatened to engulf the entire town.

Later in the year, on October 19, a two-alarm fire broke out at the Post Office Café & Cabaret at 2:45 a.m.

A decade later, another arsonist was at work. Between 2007 and 2008, twenty arson fires were set. This arsonist followed the pattern of the 1930s arsonist, often setting fires in seasonal houses where the fire was not noted and reported immediately, allowing it to spread to other houses.

Portuguese in Provincetown

When a reporter for the *Boston Globe* visited Provincetown in December 1952, he stepped into a Portuguese bakery where he heard Portuguese being spoken. Already, in 1952, this was unusual, William DeLue remarked, although 75 percent of the town was of Portuguese descent.[167]

He noted, too, that Portuguese traditions were fading as the Portuguese immigrants and their first-generation children aged or died. On Christmas Day, for example, the Portuguese used to host a town-wide open house and serve small glasses of wine and Christmas treats.

"Despite the Americanization of the Provincetown Portuguese, a portion of Provincetown's character and its vitality is still deeply Portuguese," writes Provincetown native Mary-Jo Avellar, author of *The Provincetown Portuguese Cookbook*, published in 1997 by the Provincetown Arts Press.

One way the town's Portuguese heritage has stayed alive is through its food. Back in 1952, DeLue sampled "flipper dough," and it is available today. Flipper dough is basically like a doughnut but without the hole. After rising, the dough is fried in a cast-iron frying pan, might be shaken in a bag with sugar and is served with syrup or molasses.

As an illustration of how close tourist and Portuguese Provincetown are, the Portuguese Bakery at 299 Commercial Street is recommended on *gaytravel.about.com* for its outstanding fresh pastries, breakfasts and lunches. And yes, for its flipper dough, which goes under the fancy name of *malasada*.

One Street, Many Pulitzers

What are the chances that if you happen to be a Pulitzer Prize–winning poet who subsequently wins the National Book Award, a neighbor down the street is also a Pulitzer Prize–winning poet who will scoop up the National Book Award three years after you?

The chances are good if you live on Commercial Street. We're talking, of course, about Mary Oliver, who lives in the East End of town, and Stanley Kunitz, who lived in the West End of town. (And it might be observed that three winners of the Pulitzer Prize for drama—Eugene O'Neill, Susan Glaspell and Tennessee Williams—once lived between the two. And that O'Neill also won the Nobel Prize. And that Michael Cunningham won a Pulitzer Prize for Fiction. And that Norman Mailer won Pulitzers for both fiction and nonfiction. We could go on…)

Kunitz, born in 1905 in Worcester, was awarded his Pulitzer in 1959 and his National Book Award in 1995. At the age of ninety-five, he was

Poet Stanley Kunitz (1905–2006) co-founded the Fine Arts Work Center in 1968. He is buried in Provincetown Cemetery with his third wife, Elise Asher Kunitz, a painter and poet. *Photo by the author.*

named poet laureate of the United States. He died in 2006, at the age of one hundred.

In the 1950s, Kunitz came to Provincetown with his third wife, Elise Asher, and began renting the artist Blanche Lazzell's old studio on the water at 351C Commercial Street. In 1962, Kunitz bought his own house at 32 Commercial Street because "it was so cheap!" During the more than forty summers that followed, Kunitz cultivated a garden "as a poem in stanzas" in the front of the house. "I find the combination of the gardening and the long nighttime hours at my desk to be just the right medicine for my soul," he wrote.[168] He and his wife stayed in town from June 21—their wedding anniversary and the summer solstice—until about Halloween, when they'd return to New York.

"What drew me to Provincetown was its cultural history, its reputation, after its literary and fishing origins, as a center for writers, painters, and sculptors," Kunitz wrote. "I do not know of a place that is comparable to it, with its vast seascapes, the glorious Cape light, the air that flows in from the sea, and a community of deeply engaged artists."[169]

In 1968, Kunitz was one of the founders of the Fine Arts Work Center.

As for Oliver, who was born in 1935 in Ohio, she came to Provincetown in the early 1960s with her partner, Molly Malone Cook, who ran the East End Bookshop at 349 Commercial Street. Oliver, who was awarded a Pulitzer Prize in 1984 for her book *American Primitive*, often takes Provincetown's natural world as her topic. "Something fashioned / this yellow-white lace-mass / that the sea has brought to the shore / and left—," she writes in *Something*.[170] A favorite place of Oliver is Blackwater Pond in the woods of the Province Lands. A one-mile walking trail surrounds the pond.

6
Joy in the New Millennium,
2000-2014

Your father said, while giving his toast, that, "of all my beliefs, I believe in love most."
—*Brett Every,* Beautiful Day

Governor Romney Tries to Rain on Their Wedding Day

On the morning of May 17, 2004, a dozen same-sex couples lined up on the steps of Provincetown Town Hall waiting for the doors to open at 8:00 a.m. so they could apply for marriage licenses.

May 17 was the first day that same-sex couples could marry in Massachusetts, and Massachusetts was the first state to legalize same-sex marriages. (Vermont had recognized civil unions since 2000.) By the time the day ended, fourteen same-sex couples were wed.

The previous November, the Supreme Judicial Court, in a four-to-three decision, ruled in *Goodridge v. Department of Public Health* that same-sex couples had a right to marry. "Civil Rights history was made here in 2004 when the 180-day stay on the decision of the State Judicial Court to allow same-sex marriage was lifted on May 17th," says the report of the board of selectmen in the 2004 *Town Records and Reports.* The cover of the report shows a wedding bower on the beach, draped in white wedding veil material.

Although Governor Mitt Romney tried to dampen enthusiasm for the new ruling by disallowing out-of-staters from marrying here, still they came. Two men from Alabama were the first to go through the process of applying for a license in Provincetown, driving to Orleans to request a judge waive the three-day wait, returning to Provincetown to obtain the marriage license and then finally being married by a justice of the peace.[171] One couple traveled from Santa Fe, New Mexico. "It was a joyous day," the town's selectmen concluded.

The list of marriages in the clerk's report for 2004 covers nearly eighteen full pages—over 899 same-sex couples and 25 opposite sex couples. Contrast that with 2003, when a total of 19 couples were married in Provincetown. Sometimes the town clerk's office received, in a single day, up to 150 calls and e-mails asking about the procedures for a same-sex marriage.

"On that first day our citizens, visitors and town employees all pulled together and our little town beamed brightly under the watchful eye of an interested and perplexed America," the 2004 *Town Records and Reports* noted.

At the end of the month, the selectmen decided to challenge in court the "unconstitutional and discriminatory" ban on weddings for out-of-staters. That ban was finally struck down in July 2008.

In 2012, of the 271 marriage licenses filed in Provincetown, 88 percent were for same-sex marriage, and of those, 81 percent were from out of state. Statewide, the ratio of same-sex marriages of women to men has been two to one.

A Winter Person Stays On

Jeannette de Beauvoir has officiated at many weddings in Provincetown during the past decade.

"It's a delight to marry gay and lesbian couples, many of whom have been together already for thirty, forty, even fifty years," says de Beauvoir, a writer, WOMR radio personality and ordained minister. "I derive great joy from that."[172]

De Beauvoir, who was born and raised in France's Loire Valley, earned a master's in divinity degree at Yale University. She considers herself a Catholic of the liberation school of theology, and she loves that it "gives me the opportunity to use my liturgical background and education to be with people on the best day of their lives—how cool is that?" She conducts bilingual weddings (in French and English). Her business is called GetMarriedInPTown.com.

Novelist, WOMR radio personality and ordained minister Jeannette de Beauvoir runs a business called Get Married in P'Town. *Courtesy Jeannette de Beauvoir.*

Through the years, some humorous things have occurred during her weddings—85 percent of which take place on the beach. "Two women, two wedding gowns and the beach can be an interesting combination," de Beauvoir says.

She recalls two brides from Kansas who asked de Beauvoir to plan their wedding, as well as officiate at it. "We'd gone through months of work over menus and decorations and favors," de Beauvoir says. Yet "in all that planning, it never occurred to me to tell them that stiletto heels don't work well in the sand."

About halfway down the dune at Herring Cove, one of the brides stumbled. "She grabbed her wife-to-be, who also went tumbling into one of the women attendants," de Beauvoir says. "I think by the time they reached the bottom, about six of them were involved in the mêlée." These days, de Beauvoir warns brides off stiletto heels.

And at another beach wedding, the two grooms brought their family of three large dogs to witness the ceremony. The leashed dogs were impatient as the ceremony began and wound themselves around the couple. The three leashes became so tangled that they eventually pulled down the grooms, the trellis that de Beauvoir had decorated earlier in the day, the table with the sand-ceremony vases and de Beauvoir herself.

"The dogs had the merriest time of all," she says.

De Beauvoir first came to Provincetown as a "winter person." When she was married and living in Cambridge, she'd rent an apartment on Commercial Street overlooking the harbor and watch the snow fill her deck as she sat there writing in the solitude and silence. "My first summer here was something of a shock, I have to admit," she says, referring to the crowds and the noise. Eventually, de Beauvoir bought an old sea captain's house in North Truro. "I love the desolation of winters here, and the close community that develops as a result. I am essentially a solitary person, so the 'aloneness' of the winters here works for me."

De Beauvoir says the writing community in Provincetown today is "certainly not anything that the original writers, the 'Greenwich-Village-by-the-Sea' folks, would recognize." Escalating real estate values argue against young, unknown writers casually arriving in Provincetown to write. De Beauvoir also mentions a "pecking order" among the town's writers. Some are on fellowships at the Fine Arts Work Center and keep to themselves.

Visitor Fred Howard of Ciudad Mazatlan, Sinaloa, Mexico, overlooks Provincetown Harbor with the author in August 2001. This was a month before the attack on the World Trade Center, where Howard had until recently worked. *Courtesy of the author.*

Others—nationally known, bestselling authors—"have their circles of friends and will put in local appearances at benefits for one nonprofit or another. All of this makes for a community that is at best divided and at worst nonexistent," she notes.

Still, "I realized that I felt more creative here," she says. "I think that it's partly because there are so many people here living quiet lives and simply working their art, and one cannot but feel that energy. And artists are respected here: even if one works in a shop or waits tables to pay the rent, one is still perceived primarily and fundamentally as an artist."

And yes, even in the twenty-first century, Provincetown has that special aura.

"A fishing grounds for the Wampanoag, a home for the Portuguese fleeing the Azores, a creative community for artists and writers, a place for gay and lesbian people to feel safe. Once a place has had that kind of vibe for so long, that kind of energy, it soaks in," de Beauvoir says. "Add to that the nature that surrounds and permeates it, and you have a place that feels different from any other place."

A Gallery for Provincetown

So many of Provincetown's galleries feature the work of out-of-towners that when Katherine Baltivik acquired her gallery, the Charles-Baltivik Gallery and Sculpture Garden, she decided to highlight the work of Provincetown artists.

"There were so many talented artists here that I decided I would only take those who were connected to Provincetown and limit my gallery to those people," she says, adding that her gallery is just about the only one of seventy or so to do so.

A native of Teaneck, New Jersey, Baltivik made a career in teaching language arts and in the field of Holocaust education. She also worked with the United States Holocaust Memorial Museum in Washington, D.C., producing tiles for the children's wall.[173]

With her academic schedule, she was free to spend her summers in Provincetown, and she first came during the hippie era in 1968. "I was gay, young and loved the freedom that was permitted here for my lifestyle," she says. During those early summers, she supported herself working as an artist's "shill" model, luring customers to sit for their portraits. She also sold her own mainly figurative drawings.

Artist Katherine Baltivik, owner of the Charles-Baltivik Gallery at 432 Commercial Street, poses under a gay pride flag. *Photo by Lynette Molnar.*

"At that time—yes, that early—I knew I would eventually live here," she recalls. "That became my goal as I came every summer and lived in the 'straight' world for the rest of the year." In 1970, Baltivik marched in the first Gay Pride Parade in New York, daringly only an hour distant from the school where she taught. "I was definitely influenced by my experiences in Provincetown, though the town was still changing in gay acceptance. It was still better than other places."

In 1993, twenty-five years after her first visit, Baltivik bought a small condo on Commercial Street and set her easel by a window. "I would watch the people and capture the view from my window overlooking the water," she says. "Of course, I became intrigued by the constant change of light over the water and also by the life below on the street."

The following year, she acquired her gallery "on a fluke." She had placed her work in the gallery and, when the gallery went on the market, bought it. In the early years, she continued teaching and ran the gallery during vacations. Her grueling gallery schedule revolved around twelve-hour days, seven days a week. "I built the business and opted for early retirement from teaching at the age of fifty-three, after thirty-two years," she says. By 2000, she was ready to sell her house in New York and move permanently to Provincetown.

The gallery's official address is 432 Commercial Street, but its front door opens on Kiley Court. Kiley Court used to be known as Peter Hunt's Alley, the place where Hunt ran his studio behind a sculpture garden. "I managed to view the inside of the small studio and saw a mural covering the entire back wall that he and his students painted," Baltivik says. During World War II, when Hunt's decorated recycled furniture was at the height of its popularity, Hunt snapped up every property in the alley and converted them to gift shops, studios and apartments.[174]

The Charles-Baltivik Gallery is located in Peter Hunt Alley, where Hunt's teenage employees decorated and sold his peasant furniture and accessories in the 1940s and 1950s. *Photo by the author.*

This is where, in Betty Cavanna's 1949 novel *Paintbox Summer*, a bus driver drops off seventeen-year-old Kate Vale for her summer job with Hunt. When Kate saw the "painted wood box and the hobbyhorse table" in the small courtyard, she knew she was in the right place. Here, Hunt's group of real-life artists—mainly teenage girls, including Provincetown artist Nancy Whorf—sat outside in good weather and applied Hunt's peasant designs to furniture, trays and even Christmas ornaments. Cosmetics queen Helena Rubinstein, who had a house at 42 Commercial Street from 1942 to 1947, was one of Hunt's major customers and patrons.[175] Hunt, who wrote two do-it-yourself books, had the motto: "All you need is a good brush, a can of paint, a love of color and a merry heart." He made it sound easy.

Today, Provincetown is touted as the oldest art colony in the United States. Yet its character has changed greatly from the early days of the twentieth century, when Charles Webster Hawthorne taught young artists to paint "mudheads" on the beach, and it has changed from the mid-twentieth century, when Hans Hofmann's abstract expressionism classes were at their zenith.

Painter Andrea Sawyer, who loves color, draws inspiration from Provincetown's buildings and street scenes. Her work is represented by the Charles-Baltivik Gallery. *Photo by Raeann Pacifico.*

For one thing, "Provincetown is no longer a cheap place for artists to reside," Baltivik notes, echoing de Beauvoir. In days of yore, "artists would go out on to the pier and be thrown a fish for their dinner by the Portuguese fishermen."

Two artists represented in Baltivik's gallery are Paul Cezanne, whose photographs are plays on light that capture moments at dawn or dusk and infuse them with emotion, and Andrea Sawyer, whose gorgeous oil paintings on canvas are riots of jewel tones, often slightly fuzzy, with moody reflections of color in wet streets.

"The gallery is now in its twentieth year and a tightly-knit community or family of artists is represented," Baltivik says. "All of them donate time to the gallery, painting, sitting, serving at parties. This makes them a team, rather than scattered individuals that don't know each other. Everyone works together, gives artwork for fundraisers in town and has a sense of community."

Baltivik herself paints in oil on copper, paper and wood. Provincetown's buildings and streetscapes are among her favorite subjects, and many of her paintings are infused with the blue of Provincetown's sky and sea.

"My rooftop and shoreline paintings incorporate both Provincetown and the interconnectedness of all people here," she says.

The Pilgrim Bark Park

Baltivik, who shares her home with a toy poodle named E'Behr and a mini poodle named Jacques, is among the many local artists who donated art to beautify the amazing Pilgrim Bark Park. In 2008, the nonprofit Provincetown Dog Park Association opened the dog park in a fenced, off-leash area where "dogs can run free and socialize" among works of art. Baltivik painted a large mooring ball in honor of the Portuguese heritage of the town. Ilene Charles decorated the fire hydrants so beloved by male dogs to look like "canine versions of Provincetown's police officers, firefighters and public workers." They are just outside the park on Shank Painter Road.

A few years ago, *Dog Fancy* magazine named Provincetown Dog Town USA. In 2010, the town numbered over five hundred dogs to its three thousand humans, a ratio of one to six. In January 2014, www.bringfido. com listed eight dog-friendly restaurants in town. Out-of-town dogs are also welcome in four hotels and motels, three B&Bs, 112 vacation rentals and two campgrounds. Does your dog enjoy boating? Dogs are shipping out on the Dolphin Fleet whale watches, SeaSalt Charters and Dog Gone Sailing Charters, where dogs of all sizes are fitted with doggie life vests. Leashed dogs are also welcome at Herring Cove, Race Point, Breakwater and Harbor Beaches all summer long—a boon on Cape Cod, where most towns ban dogs from the beaches for up to six months of the year.

"Pets are considered our children and are viewed by many as just that," Baltivik says. "We have CASAS[176] [animal shelter] and a number one dog park to stand as tribute to the residents' love of animals. I think people will tolerate a barking dog more than a screaming drunk."

A large doghouse stands at the entrance to the park, which was constructed on an unbuildable parcel donated by the town. The $12,500 to $15,000 annual upkeep of the park is raised solely through contributions. As befits Provincetown, many local artists have contributed sculptures to Art in the Park. These artists include Brenda Silva, a Provincetown native of Portuguese descent who painted the gorgeous Pilgrim Bark Park sign; Jody Melander, a twenty-five-year Provincetown resident who creates "backyard dream houses"; Candice Crawford, known for her whimsical sculptures; Julian Popko, whose metal dog silhouettes parade along the fence; Greg Clemco, who buries whimsical whale tails in the ground; Robert Koch, represented by the Charles-Baltivik Gallery, who created a Whale's Tail Memorial area where stones engraved in memory of departed dogs are set in a brick walkway; sculptor Chris Williams, who salutes the Native Americans

Dolphin VI, a ship with the Dolphin Fleet, which introduced whale watching to Provincetown in 1975, arrives back at MacMillan Wharf in 2003. A naturalist narrates trips to Stellwagen Bank National Marine Sanctuary. *Photo by the author.*

with a bronze sculpture of a Wampanoag casting a fishing net; Mike Kacergis, who created a large floral arrangement in metal; Nicoletta Poli, who specializes in pet paintings in her Commercial Street Gallery; and Gallery Voyeur on Commercial Street, which created large signs with photographs of dogs denoting the "Little Dogs Only" and "All Dogs" areas. In addition, Peter Stuermer donated an anchor to the gorgeously landscaped park. And guess what? In a nod to the Pilgrims, there is also a small-scale replica of the *Mayflower*.

Carnival at Land's End

On August 5, 2010, the Pilgrim Monument reached the century mark, and Provincetown celebrated in style, naturally, with a parade, concert and fireworks.

In the early part of the twentieth century, Provincetown's artists were known for partying to excess. With its potent mix of artists, bohemians and gay people, parties were creative, fun, no-holds-barred events. Take the annual parties given by the Beachcombers and the Provincetown Art Association. Back in the day, up to one thousand people attended the balls.

In 2011, the Artists' Ball was brought back in the form of the Marc Jacobs Beaux Arts Ball. Held in Provincetown Town Hall, it celebrated the recently completed, $6 million renovation of the 1896 town hall.[177] Robert Duffy, a part-time resident and president of Marc Jacobs International, underwrote the cost of the ball. Since then, it has become an annual affair, usually held around Halloween.

"Provincetown is a lascivious carnival during the summer months, and it would be a shame to miss its gaudier pleasures." Michael Cunningham writes in his 2002 paean to the town, *Land's End: A Walk Through Provincetown*.

This is a town where, if you are so inclined, you can find love in any number of places: bars that cater to various tastes, an afternoon tea dance, the parks, the dunes at Herring Cove and even a "cruisy parking lot" near town hall. And then there's a designated trysting spot on the harbor beach.

The benches in front of Provincetown Town Hall are sometimes called the "meat rack." In an attempt to "clean up" the town, the benches were removed for a time in 1971, until by popular demand they were put back. Through the years, the benches have served many purposes, and until recently they served as the "last call" spot of the night.

An estimated eight thousand "bears" thronged to Provincetown for the eleventh annual Bear Week in July 2011. Bears are a subculture of gay men "who embrace natural body hair." *Photo by Carolyn Brault Seefer.*

And then there's Spiritus Pizza at 190 Commercial Street.

As the Spiritus website tells it, "the front patio attracts the boys into making it the new meatrack, leaving the benches at Town Hall empty of late night love seekers."

Provincetown's bars close at 1:00 a.m., too early for many revelers. After last call, the patrons flock to Spiritus Pizza. In the summer, the thousand or more men standing in the street is "an orgy of sly desire; it's the world's biggest festival for loiterers," as Cunningham describes it. And meanwhile, business booms. Spiritus stays open until 2:00 a.m., selling pizza, ice cream and coffee. "Late night in Provincetown is, of course, all about sex, but the edginess that prevails in the bars and during the Spiritus hour more or less evaporates."

"You Can Get Anything You Want at Alice's Restaurant"

"I do know how to make something taste exactly as I want it," Alice May Brock says. She's sitting at a round wooden table in her gallery at 69 Commercial Street. Late morning sunlight floats into the room through pieces of stained glass displayed in the windows overlooking the street. On the table is a clutter of paintbrushes, pens and artistic accouterments. On a wall nearby are Brock's upbeat paintings of carrots, eggplants and forks and caricatures of beach-goers. She also paints beach rocks from Herring Cove.

Brock is, of course, the Alice of Alice's Restaurant in Stockbridge. Brock's pal Arlo Guthrie made her famous back in the late '60s with his song and his anti–Vietnam War movie. Brock has now lived in Provincetown for thirty-five years. She lives above the studio with her toy poodle, Amy, an elderly rescue dog whose barks punctuate the conversation.

Provincetown "is a wonderful community," she says. "I say Provincetown is where all the crackpots live. That's why I feel very comfortable here." She

Alice Brock, owner of a Stockbridge, Massachusetts restaurant, became famous with the 1969 classic film *Alice's Restaurant*. Today, she is an artist working out of a gallery at 69 Commercial Street. *Photo by the author.*

Alice Brock's colorful front door and mailbox at 69 Commercial Street suggest that an artist dwells within. *Photo by the author.*

laughs. "I'm not weird. I'm not weird at all. People can be who they want to be and it's tolerated."

When Brock first moved to Provincetown in 1979, she was "still vibrating from the restaurant business, and I didn't want to know anybody," she says. "I wanted some peace and quiet." While she found work in a restaurant, she showed up for the 2:00 a.m. shift to do prep work. "I could do it my way," she says. She concedes she is still "kind of a recluse."

Brock was conceived in Provincetown and born in Brooklyn in 1941 in the off-season. After her birth, her parents continued to summer in Provincetown. While her father ran a Christmas store for Peter Hunt, her mother "just lay in the sun all day," Brock recalls. "She had her own friends. And I was left to my own devices." The family—including Brock's sister—lived in one room behind the store. Hunt and his mother, known universally as "Ma Hunt," lived on the second floor of the house.

Ma Hunt hated Brock. "I was noisy, rude, slammed the door," she says. As for Hunt himself, "he and my father were great pals," Brock says. "My father loved art and artists. They were both bon vivants."

Brock attended Sarah Lawrence College in the late 1950s and studied philosophy with Susan Sontag. She met the architect Ray Brock in Greenwich Village and, as we all remember from *Alice's Restaurant*, later made her home in a deconsecrated church in Great Barrington that she bought for $2,000. She and Brock were working at the Stockbridge School, where Guthrie was a student. The events of the movie (which was highly fictionalized), such as Guthrie's arrest for littering on Thanksgiving, took place in the mid-'60s. Brock divorced Ray Brock and spent the 1970s running a string of restaurants.

These days, Brock is painting. "Being an artist isn't a career choice, it's a compulsion," she writes on her website. "For me, the act of creating is vital."

As a Provincetown painter, she is well aware of the town's famous light. "We all talk about the sky a lot," she says. "The cloud formations. The light is so beautiful."

On the wall is what Brock calls the "*Alice's Restaurant* Spoof Poster" that shows Brock, apparently wearing nothing but a bowler hat, tastefully situated behind a folded linen napkin, cheeks in, lips pursed and gripping a knife and fork. The poster for the movie shows Guthrie in a similar pose.

Brock pulls out a copy of the spoof poster and autographs it "Peace, Love & Rock & Roll. Alice Brock."

"There Must Be No Sorrows There"

It's frigid today in Provincetown. Twenty-nine degrees, to be exact, and the wind has numbed my fingers, despite my gloves. The grass here is brown and crunchy and, in shady spots, still covered with snow.

I'm in the presence of Norman and Norris Church Mailer, Robert Motherwell, Mary Heaton Vorse, four members of the John Whorf family, Rear Admiral Donald and Miriam MacMillan, sculptors Nanno de Groot and Avrom Sinaiko and many, many other Provincetown residents, both well known and not, each with his or her unique tale to tell. But none of them are talking. I'm standing near their graves in the new section of Provincetown Cemetery Number 2. How quiet now are the artists, writers, fishermen, explorers and hell-raisers of Provincetown!

This is—do I dare say it?—a cheerful cemetery, despite the tears shed here and the heartbreak, the regrets, the depression of grief. Some of the lots are laid out on a gentle hillside that offers a vista toward town and the Pilgrim Monument so that, unlike other melancholy and secluded cemeteries I've visited, it's not spooky at 11:00 a.m. Local people cut through Cemetery Road, and the sun is high in the sky. "There must be no sorrows there," are the words on the stone of one John Atkins, who died in 1860.

Graves reach back to the early nineteenth century, and one just wants to explore, despite the nipping cold. The north corner, back by the caretaker's shed, is the star-studded area of the dead. Acolytes regularly come here searching for Mailer's grave, a slab of white marble that's particularly hard to photograph. These fans have adorned the gravestone with shells, pens, a chewed pencil whose eraser is worn to a nub, a candle, a necklace, a small green liquor bottle and stones.

If you look hard enough, these stones, small and medium-sized stones that would nestle smoothly in the palm of your hand, are tucked away at many graves—they're here in the grass at the foot of abstract expressionist Motherwell's headstone.

So why are these loose stones set on and near the graves? Flowers are often left at graves, of course, and a glance around will reveal some stalks or, in this cold, a bright artificial poinsettia. Cut flowers wilt and die, just as the departed has done. Yet Jewish custom calls for stones at a grave site. One theory says a stone keeps the soul in place to prevent it from haunting the living. Another theory says stones are placed here because they last forever, unlike flowers, unlike life.

"While flowers may be a good metaphor for the brevity of life, stones seem better suited to the permanence of memory," David J. Wolpe writes in *Jewish Insights on Death and Mourning*. "In moments when we are faced with the fragility of life, Judaism reminds us that there is permanence amidst the pain."[178]

Mailer was buried in November 2007, with his family looking on and his son John Buffalo reading an obituary that Mailer wrote himself, joking that he had by then had fifteen divorces and sixteen wives and "I just don't feel the old vim." His sixth and final wife, Norris Church Mailer, to whom he was married for twenty-seven years, sat under a green tent that day. "And who knows what Norman is doing on the other side? I'm curious to catch up with him and find out," Norris Mailer wrote at the end of *A Ticket to the Circus*. Three years and eleven days after Mailer's death, she joined her husband under the white stone.

A few paces away is the grave of Motherwell, with Motherwell's famous signature affixed to the headstone with a bronze plaque. Motherwell died of a stroke in an ambulance on the way to Cape Cod Hospital on July 16, 1991. He was seventy-six. In life, Motherwell lived two doors down from Mailer on Commercial Street. When Motherwell's family held his memorial service out on the beach, Mailer merely had to step outside his own door, into the sand, to join several hundred other mourners.

A few steps from Motherwell's grave are those of Pulitzer Prize–winning poet Stanley Kunitz and his wife, Elise Asher Kunitz. Kunitz and Motherwell were among the founders of the Fine Arts Work Center in 1968.

"He Loved the Earth So Much, He Wanted to Stay Forever" are the words etched on Kunitz's stone. He died on May 14, 2006, at age one hundred.

The Ghost Train

Sometimes in the quiet, just after midnight or in the still hours before dawn, residents hear a train passing through. They feel the vibrations of the big Diesel engine, hear the rhythmic *click-clack* of the wheels racing along the tracks, hear the horn.

The Old Colony Railroad reached Provincetown in 1873; the trouble is, passenger service to the Cape's tip ended in 1938, and freight service ran until 1960, when the tracks were abandoned. Skeptics say the noises are a steamroller on Route 6, the hum of a generator, trucks loading trash at the landfill.

The Old Colony train ran to Provincetown from 1873 until all service ended in 1960. Some residents still hear a ghost train passing through. *Painting by Deane Folsom Sr.*

It is hard to say what makes this end of Cape Cod so strange. You don't have to be a religious person to concede, as the flashes from the Aurora Borealis stain the night sky green, that the mysteries in this universe of ours are many.

We are born, we love, we grieve, we die. The world changes.

There are no trains here anymore. These are ghost trains.

"The timelines and dimensions of the old paradigm are collapsing," one woman assured the witnesses. "The train is real, as real as you are."

In 1886, town crier George Washington Ready claimed he saw a sea serpent at Herring Cove. While most have treated the incident as a result of Ready's love of the bottle, we wonder.

We truly wonder.

Notes

Chapter 1

1. buildingprovincetown.wordpress.com, search for "Motherwell."
2. *Provincetown Advocate*, March 19, 1942.
3. Vorse, *Time and the Town*, 337.
4. Garrison, *Mary Heaton Vorse*, 295.
5. *Provincetown Advocate*, January 4, 1940.
6. Ibid., February 29, 1940.
7. *Town Records and Reports*, 1940.
8. *Provincetown Advocate*, June 18, 1942.
9. Devlin, *Selected Letters of Tennessee Williams*, vol. 1, 262.
10. *Provincetown Advocate*, September 12, 1940.
11. Ibid., May 19, 1938.
12. Meyers, *Edmund Wilson*, 231.
13. Devlin, *Selected Letters of Tennessee Williams*, vol. 1, 322.
14. Ibid., 327–28.
15. *Mirages*, Kindle edition.
16. *Provincetown Advocate*, December 11, 1941.
17. Ibid., December 18, 1941.
18. Hollis Taggart Galleries, *From Hawthorne to Hofmann*, 71.
19. Dearborn, *Mistress of Modernism*, 191.
20. buildingprovincetown.wordpress.com, search for "Motherwell."
21. *Provincetown Advocate*, September 9, 1942.
22. *Town Records and Reports*, 1941.
23. Devlin, *Selected Letters of Tennessee Williams*, vol. 1, 529.
24. *Provincetown Advocate*, September 28, 1944.

25. Ibid., September 21, 1944.
26. Kaplan, *Tennessee Williams in Provincetown*, 57.
27. Interview with Robert Harrison, October 31, 2013.
28. Goodman, *Hofmann*, 7.
29. Sandler, *A Sweeper-Up After Artists*, 85.
30. Goodman, *Hofmann*, 25.
31. Ibid., 41.
32. Ibid., 30.
33. Levin, *Lee Krasner*, 122.
34. Kuh, *My Love Affair with Modern Art*, 248.
35. Goodman, *Hofmann*, 104.
36. Three generations of the Welsh family of Provincetown sat on the district court bench. The line began with Walter in 1914, continued to Robert Sr. and passed to Robert Jr., who served from 1973 to 2008, when he retired, according to the *Cape Cod Times*, February 4, 2008.
37. *Provincetown Advocate*, July 10, 1947.
38. Berger, *Cape Cod Pilot*, 263.
39. *Provincetown Advocate*, August 19, 1937.
40. Ibid., August 16, 1945.
41. Kaplan, *Tennessee Williams in Provincetown*, 82.
42. Ibid., 62.
43. R. Wilson, *To the Life of the Silver Harbor*, 69.
44. E. Wilson, *The Forties*, 221.
45. *Provincetown Advocate*, July 1, 1948.
46. Kees, *Weldon Kees and the Midcentury Generation*, 113.

Chapter 2

47. Kees, *Weldon Kees and the Midcentury Generation*, 154.
48. *Provincetown Advocate*, June 5, 1952.
49. Wright, *Provincetown*, Vol. II, 118. Robert Harrison said Baiona always had a theatrical bent. On Labor Day weekend, he would arrive at Herring Cove in a speedboat and parade up and down the beach proclaiming himself the "king of Provincetown." Someone invariably corrected him, saying, "You're not the king, you're the queen."
50. *Provincetown Advocate*, August 4, 1960.
51. Ibid., July 20, 1950.
52. *New York Times*, July 3, 1949.
53. Reidel, *Vanished Act*, 198.
54. Hunt, *Peter Hunt's Cookbook*, 172.
55. *Provincetown Advocate*, May 23, 1940.
56. R. Wilson, *To the Life of the Silver Harbor*, 164.
57. Hunt, *Peter Hunt's Cookbook*, 111.
58. Garrison, *Mary Heaton Vorse*, 320.

59. R. Wilson, *To the Life of the Silver Harbor*, 159.

60. *New York Times*, September 19, 1988.

61. *Provincetown Advocate*, August 22, 1957.

62. Chrysler Art Museum, *Controversial Century*.

63. *New York Times*, February 8, 1978.

Chapter 3

64. Dearborn, *Mailer*, 156. Dearborn offers an excellent description of Mailer's complex relationship with Roy Cohn.

65. Ibid., 158.

66. Ibid., 156.

67. *Provincetown Advocate*, September 2, 1954.

68. Ibid., August 11, 1960.

69. Brevda, *Harry Kemp*, 207.

70. R. Wilson, *Near the Magician*, 76.

71. *Boston Globe*, December 10, 12, 1952.

72. Brevda, *Harry Kemp*, 217.

73. *Provincetown Advocate*, July 26, 1962.

74. Andersen, *Those Few Precious Days*, 305–6.

75. *Provincetown Advocate*, July 9, 1959.

76. Ibid., April 2, 1959, letter to editor by Miriam DeWitt of Washington, D.C., who first visited in 1911.

77. *Provincetown Advocate*, May 21, 1959.

78. *Town Records and Reports*, 1961.

79. http://users.rcn.com/rayzrealm/doclib/misstime.txt.

80. Boulton, *Part of a Long Story*, 258 fn.

81. *New York Times*, July 24, 1963.

82. *Boston Globe*, March 1, 2004.

83. Kelly, *Feast or Famine*, 86.

84. Information on Waters comes from a 2011 interview with Gerald Peary. www.geraldpeary.com/interviews/wxyz/waters-p-town.html.

85. *Boston Globe*, March 9, 1969.

86. *New York Times*, June 26, 1966.

87. *Cape Cod Times*, February 24, 2005.

88. Manso, *P'Town*, 118.

89. *Provincetown Advocate*, September 23, 1965.

90. *Boston Globe*, December 15, 1952.

91. *Provincetown Advocate*, April 21, 1966.

92. Ibid., April 7, 1966.

93. Geldzahler, *Hans Hofmann*, 11, 13.

94. *New York Times*, February 18, 1966.

95. Meryman, *Andrew Wyeth*, 414.

96. *New York Daily News*, July 19, 2001.

97. *Artnet News*, July 19, 2001.

98. Garrison, *Mary Heaton Vorse*, 327.

99. *New York Times*, June 15, 1966.

100. Garrison, *Mary Heaton Vorse*, 325.

101. *Provincetown Advocate*, May 27, 1965.

102. Steve Barrie, "Steve's Own Corner," *Provincetown Advocate*, April 30, 1964.

103. *Provincetown Advocate*, August 27, 1964.

104. Ibid., June 24, 1965.

105. Ibid., July 8, 1965.

106. *San Francisco Chronicle* columnist Herb Caen is credited with bringing the word "hippie" into widespread use in January 1967.

107. *New York Times*, September 9, 1965.

108. Kelly, *Feast or Famine*, 54.

109. *Provincetown Advocate*, June 16, 1966.

110. *New York Times*, July 25, 1966.

111. Warhol and Hackett, *POPism*, 179.

112. Bockris, *Up-Tight*, 53.

113. Warhol and Hackett, *POPism*, 179. Warhol devotes a page and a half to the long weekend in Provincetown.

114. *Provincetown Advocate*, May 25, 1967.

115. Information on Townsend comes from Shand-Tucci, *Crimson Letter*, 236–40.

116. http://www.geraldpeary.com/interviews/wxyz/waters-p-town.html.

117. *Provincetown Advocate*, December 7, 1967.

118. Kelly, *Feast or Famine*, 56.

119. http://web.fawc.org/overview-and-history.

120. *New York Times*, November 11, 1968.

121. Dearborn, *Norman Mailer*, 278.

122. Much of this information comes from Damore's 678-page book *In His Garden*. The title comes from Costa's habit of inviting young women to see his marijuana patch in the Truro woods, where the bodies were found.

123. *New York Times*, March 6, 1969.

124. Damore, *In His Garden*, 37.

125. *Boston Globe*, March 9, 1969.

126. Damore, *In His Garden*, 113.

127. Vonnegut, *Wampeters Foma & Granfalloons*, 67.

128. Ibid., xxvi.

129. *Boston Globe*, May 15, 1970. My family had two minor connections with the case. In the 1970s, our electrician in Providence, Rhode Island, was Joe Walsh, brother of Patricia Walsh. Later, my parents bought a house in Chatham across the street from a member of Costa's defense team, Justin Cavanaugh.

130. Vonnegut, *Wampeters Foma & Granfalloons*, 68.

131. Preston, *Franny: The Queen of Provincetown*, 60.

Chapter 4

132. Interview with Wendy Hackett Everett, December 2, 2010.

133. Kelly, *Feast or Famine*, 99.

134. Ibid., 103.

135. Ibid., 80.

136. *New York Times*, March 16, 1971.

137. *Cape Cod Standard-Times*, July 23, 1972.

138. www.castlehill.org.

139. Killen, *1973 Nervous Breakdown*, 2.

140. Ibid., 8.

141. Bourdain, *Kitchen Confidential*, 20.

142. Ibid., 25.

143. Ibid., 27.

144. Ibid., 28–29.

145. *Boston Globe*, December 22, 1974.

146. *New York Times*, February 17, 1983.

147. www.ptown.org.

148. *New York Times*, July 20, 1981.

Chapter 5

149. www.AIDS.gov.

150. *Boston Globe*, June 23, 1983.

151. Shilts himself would die of AIDS on February 17, 1994.

152. Shilts, *And the Band Played On*, 12.

153. www.wickedlocal.com, April 22, 2009.

154. www.capecodonline.com, April 26, 2009.

155. www.prx.org. Search for "There Were Ghosts Everywhere: An Oral History of AIDS in Provincetown," by independent producer Sarah Yahm. This is a twelve-minute audio piece on the town's response to AIDS.

156. *Boston Globe*, August 16, 1987.

157. Ibid., March 27, 1988.

158. www.AIDS.gov.

159. Skillings, *How Many Die*, 36.

160. www.capecodonline.com, April 26, 2009.

161. Dearborn, *Norman Mailer*, 384.

162. Ibid., 384, details on relationship and real estate, 380 ff. Interestingly, Roy Cohn is not found in J. Michael Lennon's *Norman Mailer: A Double Life* (2013).

163. buildingprovincetown.wordpress.com, search for 625 Commercial Street.

164. Dearborn, *Norman Mailer*, 386.

165. Associated Press, October 17, 1987.

166. capecodfd.com/pages%20depts/21%20fd%20%20provincetown.htm.

167. *Boston Globe*, December 15, 1952.

168. Kunitz, *The Wild Braid*, 42–43.

169. Ibid., 41–42.
170. Oliver, *Why I Wake Early*, 38.

Chapter 6

171. *New York Times*, May 18, 2004.
172. Interview with Jeannette de Beauvoir, October 14, 2013.
173. Interview with Katherine Baltivik, October 26, 2013.
174. Van Dine, *The Search for Peter Hunt*, 179.
175. Peter Hunt moved out of Provincetown in the 1960s, and by the time of his death in 1967, his work was no longer in vogue. Today, Hunt's painted designs are highly collectible and are often auctioned at places like Eldred's Auctioneers in Dennis.
176. The Carrie A. Seaman Animal Shelter on Sandy Hill Lane, Provincetown, is a no-kill shelter "designed to support the wonderful animals of lower Cape Cod."
177. *Cape Cod Times*, September 5, 2011.
178. Riemer, *Jewish Insights on Death and Mourning*, 129.

Bibliography

Books on Provincetown and Its People

Abell, Mary Ellen. *Long Point: An Artists' Place (1977–1998)*. Provincetown, MA: Provincetown Art Association and Museum, 2012.

Berger, Josef. *Cape Cod Pilot: A WPA Guide*. Boston: Northeastern University Press, 1985.

Boulton, Agnes. *Part of a Long Story*. New York: Doubleday & Company, Inc., 1958.

Brevda, William. *Harry Kemp: The Last Bohemian*. Cranbury, NJ: Associated University Presses, 1986.

Cavanna, Betty. *Paintbox Summer*. Philadelphia: Westminster Press, 1949.

Chrysler Art Museum. *The Controversial Century: 1850–1950. Paintings from the Collection of Walter P. Chrysler, Jr*. Provincetown, MA: Chrysler Art Museum, 1962.

Cozzi, Ciro. *Ciro & Sal's Cookbook*. New York: Donald I. Fine, Inc., 1987.

Crotty, Frank. *Provincetown Profiles: And Others on Cape Cod*. Barre, MA: Barry Gazette, 1958.

Cunningham, Michael. *Land's End: A Walk Through Provincetown*. New York: Crown Publishers, 2002.

Damore, Leo. *In His Garden: The Anatomy of a Murderer*. New York: Arbor House, 1981.

Dearborn, Mary V. *Mailer: A Biography*. Boston: Houghton Mifflin Company, 1999.

———. *Mistress of Modernism: The Life of Peggy Guggenheim*. New York: Houghton Mifflin Company, 2004.

Devlin, Albert J., and Nancy M. Tischler, eds. *The Selected Letters of Tennessee Williams*. Vol. I, *1920–1945*. New York: New Directions, 2000.

Garrison, Dee. *Mary Heaton Vorse: The Life of an American Insurgent*. Philadelphia: Temple University Press, 1989.

Geldzahler, Henry. *Hans Hofmann: The Renate Series*. New York: Metropolitan Museum of Art, 1972.

Goodman, Cynthia. *Hofmann*. New York: Abbeville Press, 1986.

BIBLIOGRAPHY

Hollis Taggart Galleries. *From Hawthorne to Hofmann: Provincetown Vignettes, 1899–1945*. New York: Hollis Taggart Galleries, 2003.

Hopkins, Budd. *Art, Life and UFOs*. New York: Anomalist Books, 2009. Kindle edition.

Hunt, Peter. *Peter Hunt's Cape Cod Cookbook*. New York: Gramercy Publishing Co., 1954.

Kaplan, David. *Tennessee Williams in Provincetown*. East Brunswick, NJ: Hansen Publishing Group, 2007.

Kees, Weldon, and Robert E. Knoll, eds. *Weldon Kees and the Midcentury Generation: Letters, 1935–1955*. Lincoln: University of Nebraska Press, 2003.

Kelly, Julia Whorf. *Feast or Famine: Growing Up Bohemian in Provincetown*. Stuart, FL: Julia Whorf Kelly, 2008.

Kemp, Harry. *Love Among the Cape Enders*. New York: Macaulay Company, 1931.

Kittredge, Henry C. *Cape Cod: Its People and Their History*. 2nd edition. Boston: Houghton Mifflin Company, 1968.

Krahulik, Karen Christel. *Provincetown: From Pilgrim Landing to Gay Resort*. New York: New York University Press, 2005.

Kunitz, Stanley. *The Wild Braid: A Poet Reflects on a Century in the Garden*. New York: W.W. Norton & Company, 2005.

Lawless, Debra. *Provincetown: A History of Artists and Renegades in a Fishing Village*. Charleston, SC: The History Press, 2011.

Lennon, J. Michael, ed. *Norman Mailer: A Double Life*. New York: Simon & Schuster, 2013.

———. *Norman Mailer's Provincetown: The Wild West of the East*. Provincetown, MA: Provincetown Arts Press, 2005

Levin, Gail. *Lee Krasner: A Biography*. New York: William Morrow, 2011.

Mailer, Norman. *Tough Guys Don't Dance*. New York: Random House, 1984.

Mailer, Norris Church. *A Ticket to the Circus: A Memoir*. New York: Random House Trade Paperbacks, 2011.

Manso, Peter. *Ptown: Art, Sex and Money on the Outer Cape*. New York: Scribner, 2002.

Meyers, Jeffrey. *Edmund Wilson: A Biography*. New York: Cooper Square Press, 2003.

Myrer, Anton. *Evil Under the Sun*. New York: Random House, 1951.

Nin, Anais. *Mirages: The Unexpurgated Diary of Anais Nin 1939–1947*. Edited by Paul Herron. San Antonio, TX: Sky Blue Press, 2013. Kindle edition.

Oliver, Mary. *House of Light*. Boston: Beacon Press, 1990.

———. *Why I Wake Early*. Boston: Beacon Press, 2004.

Preston, John. *Franny: The Queen of Provincetown*. Vancouver, BC: Arsenal Pulp Press, 2005.

Provincetown Art Association and Museum. *The Provocative Years, 1935–1945: The Hans Hofmann School and Its Students in Provincetown*. Provincetown, MA: Provincetown Art Association and Museum, 1990.

Reidel, James. *Vanished Act: The Life and Art of Weldon Kees*. Lincoln: University of Nebraska Press, 2003.

Sandler, Irving. *A Sweeper-Up After Artists: A Memoir*. New York: Thames & Hudson, 2003.

Skillings, R.D. *How Many Die*. Hanover, NH: University Press of New England, 2001.

Town Records and Reports of the Town Officers of Provincetown, Mass. Provincetown, MA: Advocate Press, published annually.

Vonnegut, Kurt, Jr. *Wampeters Foma & Granfalloons*. New York: Delacorte Press, 1974.

Vorse, Mary Heaton. *Time and the Town: A Provincetown Chronicle*. Provincetown, MA: Cape Cod Pilgrim Memorial Association, 1990.

BIBLIOGRAPHY

Williams, Tennessee. *Memoirs*. New York: Doubleday & Company, Inc., 1975.

Wilson, Edmund. *The Fifties: From Notebooks and Diaries of the Period*. New York: Farrar, Straus and Giroux, 1986.

———. *The Forties: From Notebooks and Diaries of the Period*. New York: Farrar, Straus and Giroux, 1984.

Wilson, Reuel K. *To the Life of the Silver Harbor: Edmund Wilson and Mary McCarthy on Cape Cod*. Hanover, NH: University Press of New England, 2008.

Wilson, Rosalind Baker. *Near the Magician: A Memoir of My Father, Edmund Wilson*. New York: Grove Weidenfeld, 1989.

Wright, John Hardy. *Provincetown*. Vol. II. Charleston, SC: Arcadia Publishing, 1998.

Website

buildingprovincetown.wordpress.com [This useful and informative illustrated website is searchable by addresses, names, words and buildings and is the precursor to the forthcoming book *Building Provincetown*. The book is to be published in the fall of 2014, a date that will coincide with the centennial celebration of the Provincetown Art Association and Museum. The author is David W. Dunlap, a veteran *New York Times* reporter whose father was an architect.]

Other Helpful Sources

Andersen, Christopher. *These Few Precious Days: The Final Year of Jack with Jackie*. New York: Simon & Schuster, Inc., 2013.

Bockris, Victor, and Gerard Malanga. *Up-Tight: The Velvet Underground Story*. New York: Omnibus Press, 1983.

Bourdain, Anthony. *Kitchen Confidential: Adventures in the Culinary Underbelly*. New York: Bloomsbury, 2000.

Cather, Willa. *Not Under Forty*. New York: A.A. Knopf, 1936.

Doane, Doris. *A Book of Cape Cod Houses*. Boston: David R. Godine, 2000.

Killen, Andreas. *1973 Nervous Breakdown: Watergate, Warhol, and the Birth of Post-Sixties America*. New York: Bloomsbury Publishing, 2006.

Kuh, Katharine. *My Love Affair with Modern Art: Behind the Scenes with a Legendary Curator*. New York: Arcade Publishing, 2006.

Kurlansky, Mark. *1968: The Year that Rocked the World*. New York: Ballantine Books, 2004.

Meryman, Richard. *Andrew Wyeth: A Secret Life*. New York: Harper Perennial, 1998.

Riemer, Jack, ed. *Jewish Insights on Death and Mourning*. New York: Schocken Books, 1995. [Wolpe's essay is "Why Stones Instead of Flowers?"]

Shand-Tucci, Douglass. *The Crimson Letter: Harvard, Homosexuality, and the Shaping of American Culture*. New York: St. Martin's Griffin, 2003.

Shilts, Randy. *And the Band Played On: Politics, People, and the AIDS Epidemic*. New York: St. Martin's Press, 1987.

Warhol, Andy, and Pat Hackett. *POPism: The Warhol '60s*. New York: Harcourt Brace Jovanovich, 1980.

About the Author

D ebra Lawless is a freelance
writer living on Cape Cod. She
earned a BA in history and classics
from Stanford University and an MS
in journalism from Boston University
and holds a certificate in Boston
University's Genealogical Research
Program. A native of Providence,
Rhode Island, she has published
numerous articles in the *Cape Cod
Chronicle*, *Cape Cod* magazine and
Chatham magazine. Her previous
books are *Provincetown: A History of
Artists and Renegades in a Fishing Village*,
Chatham in the Jazz Age and *Chatham:
From the Second World War to the Age
of Aquarius*. She also contributed a
chapter to *Three Centuries in a Cape Cod
Village: The Story of Chatham*.

Photo by Stuart Stearns.